ALLY AND ME: THE INTEGRATION OF SPIRIT AND FORM

ALLY AND ME: THE INTEGRATION OF SPIRIT AND FORM

By
Purandev Kaur

ISBN: 9781688012684 (paperback)

This book is dedicated to my sister, Allison Lynn Willen, my traveling companion—in this world and the next.

The connection between sisters can never be broken.

I love you, Allison.

Travel isn't always pretty. It isn't always comfortable. Sometimes it hurts, it even breaks your heart. But that's okay. The journey changes you; it should change you. It leaves marks on your memory, on your consciousness, on your heart, and on your body. You take something with you. Hopefully, you leave something good behind.

—Anthony Bourdain

TABLE OF CONTENTS

FOREWORD

You are about to experience one of the most beautiful love stories I have ever read. *Ally and Me: The Integration of Spirit and Form* is a remarkably insightful book, dedicated to the author's younger sister, Ally Willen, who lost her life during a flash flood while hiking in Mount Aspiring National Park in New Zealand. She was just 20 years old at the time of her transition. It boggles the mind how someone such as Ally, so young, vibrant, and seemingly full of promise could be taken from us so prematurely.

When faced with a tragedy of this magnitude, how do we respond to such an injustice of nature? How do we purify our thoughts in such a way to discover the hidden lessons to be gleaned, all the while enduring such excruciating pain and turmoil?

Unbeknownst to the author, Purandev Kaur, her spirit guides for years had been preparing her for one of the most horrific storms imaginable. Along the way, she became enlightened to the expression of distilled consciousness. In her book she will share with us her journey out of the abyss with the help of many miracles and illuminations offered to her by the Universe.

As my dear friend, Dr. Wayne Dyer often said: "When you change the way you look at things, the things you look at change." Purandev Kaur, while navigating her course, has changed the thought, coming to appreciate the deathless nature of those with an enlightened mind.

Many have shared with me their concern that if a major catastrophe were to occur in their lives, the sum of their fears would leave them in a place where they wouldn't be able to handle it.

I am reminded of an event that occurred back in September of 1977, the beginning of my second year in medical school. The summer had been had been a soggy one for Kansas City as yet another intense storm front headed our way. In less than twenty-four hours, 12 inches of rain was dumped on the saturated city.

Within hours, Brush Creek, normally a mere trickle of a stream, rose twenty-one feet. Flash flooding produced a torrent of raging water smashing into everything in its path. In an instant, underground-parking garages became submerged in the murky, debris-filled water. Storefront windows imploded from the pressure of the waves crashing into them.

I was perched on the peak of a stone bridge that arched over the creek, a passive witness to this awesome expression of unleashed power by Mother Nature. I watched as large trees were easily uprooted, tossed downstream like matchsticks. The raging water engulfed everything in its wake. Nineteen people lost their lives in those few minutes of that fateful day, swept away into the roaring, wild wall of water.

Many times since I have found myself reflecting on that frightening and deadly rampage. I have often contemplated the important metaphor offered by that event: A bridge over troubled waters.

We consider ourselves fortunate as we lollygag along, savoring life, accruing pleasurable experiences here and there. There is no question that smooth sailing can be a marvelous experience. Its enjoyment should be appreciated to the fullest. But at some point, the calm waters of life will become tumultuous and unsettled. Occasionally, they may rage out of control; setbacks and obstacles will be encountered. Deep and wide crevasses might appear before us replacing our previously safe path, threatening our passage to the other side of the canyon.

We apprehensively peer over the edge of the precipice,

perilously looking down at the rapids slicing into the floodwaters. We hope against all odds that we will not lose our footing. We pray that we won't fall into the turbulence below.

As the pressure surges, the waves begin lapping up against us and steadily rise higher and higher grabbing at us, threatening to engulf us.

Oh, it would be nice if we could avoid such turmoil and the suffering and fear generated by it. But sorrow, sadness, disease and loss are all part of life as we know it in the material world. The challenge is to find a way to navigate through these seemingly difficult experiences. The question becomes how do we bridge the divide over such troubled waters? How does we learn from such apparently negative experiences? And are they really negative experiences?

My personal truth is that there is no such thing as a negative experience. If we can learn even a small lesson from an horrific incident, it no longer remains a negative encounter; it has become a positive one.

When faced with adversity, it is how we respond to the difficulty that determines who we are. Our life experiences will become calamitous only if we make the conscious decision to make tragedies out of them. We might just as easily choose to view them as opportunities for personal growth.

The inherent difficulties and dangers can become the driving force of change. The more daunting the challenge and the greater the apparent obstacle, the more potential there is for enlightenment.

Rather than lamenting the troubled waters we encounter, we can choose to be grateful for them. Purandev Kaur has learned and shares with the reader how these obstacles in life can become a source of strength, empowering us to rise above the very adversity that appears to obstruct our way. We can embrace these tumultuous times and challenges, accepting them as gifts from the Divine. By being grateful for the raging river that blocks our way, we can use the experience to bridge the gap from turmoil, disappointment, and suffering to a place of understanding, wisdom and insight.

The falls of our lives provide the energy for us to be propelled to a place of higher consciousness. That concept originally came from the Kabbalah, the ancient mystical text of Judaism.

When life is cushy, not a lot of growth occurs. In order to progress and mature spiritually, life and its challenges will necessarily have to become more challenging. The more daunting the challenges and the greater the apparent obstacles, the more potential there is for personal growth.

Consider the analogy of weight training, the sole purpose of which is to enhance the contractile fibers of one's muscle mass. The body breaks down and rebuilds every single one of its muscles every fifteen to thirty days. Weight lifting accelerates that process. Science has demonstrated that resistance-training causes break down of muscle, which ultimately culminates in increased growth, muscle mass and strength. This occurs as a direct result of the healing process that occurs during the days following the exertion.

In other words, the muscle fibers must be broken down to their elemental parts before they can be rebuilt into a form much stronger than they had been before. The only way however for this to occur is allow adequate time for recovery. If one resumes the exercise too early, further degradation of muscle will occur which ultimately results in further weakening. This healing process requires the tincture of time.

So it is with us as well. There are times when we must be broken down to the core in order to be able to rebuild to a place where we come to find the new structure so much stronger than the old one. The recovery from such a metamorphosis often takes tincture of time. From Ernest Hemingway: *"Life breaks all of us, but some of us are stronger in the broken places."*

In this, we have one of two choices. We can either resist, becoming the victim or we can accept what is placed before us on our plate. If we choose to view the crap that happens to us as opportunities for personal growth, the difficult days, as Purandev Kaur illustrates in her book, can become the driving force of major change. But know that such epiphanies are invariably offered to us through the agony of life. The very life experience that caused so much pain can become the actual vehicle of deliverance.

It is the falls of our life, the heart ache that we endure that like a heavy wrecking ball, breaks down old resistant foundations and attitudes in which we had become entrenched, allowing us to progress onto a higher plateau of awakening. In letting go of the attachment, these crumbling structures open up a space, revealing realty ready for our own inner urban renewal of spirit.

Carl Perkins once said, *"If it weren't for the rocks in its bed, the stream would have no song."* Such is the effect of obstacles along our path . . . they actually enrich the experience.

You are about to read a life-changer. Purandev Kaur encourages the reader not to delay enlightenment. She knows, after all, that it already lies within us. It's just that we have forgotten who we are, why we came back and what is our purpose.

As a piece of God, this spiritual wisdom belongs as much to us as it does to everything else in the Universe. It's just a matter of recognizing our history once again. *Ally and Me* will help you traverse your bridge over troubled waters.

That Ally ended up in New Zealand was no mistake. In fact, it was quite purposeful. She was on a personal mission of seeking and discovery.

Her ascension occurred on Mount *Aspiring* National Park. Where else could it have unfolded?

Namaste,

~ Dr. Terry Gordon
Author of *No Storm Lasts Forever*
Transforming Suffering Into Insight

A Note from Purandev

This is a deeply personal story.

It is a deeply personal story about my sister and it is also a deeply personal and vulnerable account of my own healing journey.

Five years ago on April 24th, 2015, my sister Ally transitioned from this life. She revealed to me after her passing that she and I would write a book together. The book, she said, would be a collaboration between us that would serve to provide humanity with a message of love and comfort about the transition to the other side. Of course I fervently agreed to write the book with my sister, for I would have—and still would—do anything for her. Little did I know at the time, however, what this book would ask of me.

This book has asked me to open the chamber of my heart and pour it onto these pages with relentless vulnerability. It has asked me to conduct a raw and honest inventory of my deepest fears and insecurities and then expose them to the world. It has asked me to step into territory I would rather avoid because it meant exposing some of my deepest fears—fears of my failure, fears of my success, and fears of being seen for who I truly am.

In those moments of fear and trepidation, I recalled my sister's tenacity and her resolve to say "yes" to every challenge that life handed to her. Several days before my sister died, she went skydiving in New Zealand. There is a picture of her with her arms sprawled wide, free-falling into the air, trusting that she would be carried through. In my own way, this book is my version of skydiving.

It is with this preface in mind that I give you my story. This book has asked me to summon my courage and share with you those things I have feared sharing the most: my misdiagnosis of bipolar disorder as a child, my acceptance of my intuitive abilities, and my debilitating journey with grief after experiencing the death of my sister. In sharing these experiences, I am reminded that I am not as isolated as I sometimes believe myself to be, for many of us can undoubtably relate to these experiences in some way. In sharing my story, I am also reminded of the importance of breaking the silence and the stigma surrounding such topics. Sensitive and intuitive people need to be told that they are not alone and that they are loved and celebrated for who they are; grieving mothers, fathers, siblings, and friends need to be reminded that there are others who have gone before them on this journey of healing and who have come out the other side; and all of us need to remember that truly, we are embarking on the journey of life together.

My story is your story, as your story is mine. In actuality there is no separation between us. Yet we are also each individuals, with our own unique experiences, beliefs, and perspectives. What I am offering here is one viewpoint that was formulated through my own experiences—nothing less and nothing more. My hope is that you will take what fits for you and leave the rest, for there are many paths to truth. Indeed, it is the contrast of our varying perspectives that adds richness to the fabric of life.

May me and Ally's story serve to awaken you to the beauty of your own journey.

With love,

Purandev Kaur

INTRODUCTION

Purandev Kaur

It was an overcast and rainy autumn day in Norfolk, VA where my apartment overlooked the boats that docked the sea like giant nautical guards. A gentle mist coated the outside of my bedroom window, obscuring my view. Above me, rain knocked softly on the ceiling, announcing its humble arrival.

Cradled by the ambiance of the misty afternoon, I stared at the e-mail on my computer screen, proudly announcing my new name in bold letters: Purandev Kaur.

I repeated the words softly on my tongue, exploring the texture of them for the first time. "Purandev Kaur," I whispered, as though I was tasting the flavor of each syllable.

The email from the spiritual organization that had granted me my new name explained it all: *Puran* meant whole or complete. *Dev* meant angelic or divine. Together the syllables of my new name, which was given in the Gurmukhi language, meant, "She who embodies wholeness when she experiences God-consciousness."

It was to be my spiritual name, granted to me from the lineage of kundalini yoga. Having been on a path of spiritual study and exploration for several years, I had recently requested that I be given my spiritual name as an initiation into deeper levels of connection with my higher self and my higher purpose.

And here it was; it had finally arrived.

It felt as though I had been awaiting this moment for decades. Eager to share this special occasion with someone, my mind quickly scanned a list of people to call—and in a heartbeat reached the only logical conclusion: I had to call my sister, Ally. She was, in fact, the only person who I could call, because she was the only person who would truly understand my new name and what it meant for me to receive it.

My fingers quickly found her contact information on my phone. "Ally!" I breathlessly exclaimed once she answered. "Guess what—I got my spiritual name!"

"What!" she cried, her breath catching audibly in her throat as her excitement rose to match my own. "Tell me, what is it?"

"It's Purandev Kaur!" I said, savoring the opportunity to speak my name aloud for the first time and to share it with my sister.

"Well, I don't know what it means, but it's beautiful," she said. Listening to her in that moment, I was struck by how much our voices sounded alike. I recalled that while we were growing up, people could never tell us apart when we answered the phone—often mistaking me for Ally and Ally for me.

"Thank you, Sissy," I said, referring to my nickname for her. "I wanted to tell you first."

"I'm honored," Ally said. I could feel her smiling. Although she was hundreds of miles away at college, in that moment there was no distance between us; it was as though we were sharing the same voice, the same name, the same heart.

And so it was on that day that I left behind my given name as Emily Willen and adopted my spiritual name as Purandev Kaur—a moment I was blessed to share with my sister Ally, only a mere six months before devastation struck and changed my life forever.

When She Fell...
There are few things in this life that have the ability to shake you to your core with the ferocity of an earthquake. When such significant life events occur, they often seem to happen outside the

realm of linear time. They remain frozen in our hearts and memories like tiny icicles inside of us, until the long process of healing begins to take place and finally starts to thaw them out.

In my case, the frozen memory occurred on the afternoon of April 24, 2015, when I received a voicemail message from my mother informing me that Ally was missing. I was in the car, running errands near my apartment in Norfolk, Virginia, where I was living after obtaining my master's degree as an art therapist. I glanced down at my phone, noting that my mother had left me a voicemail. I almost decided to listen to it later, but something prompted me not to wait.

The sound of my mother's voice on the other end of the phone froze my circulation and halted my breathing. "Honey," she said in the message, "you need to call home immediately. We just got a message that Ally went on a hike yesterday, and she's missing."

An image of my sister's face engulfed my mind like a movie screen. I saw her light-brown hair, chopped short to her chin now—over the years she had grown it long and cut it, donating her locks to help make wigs for people going through chemotherapy. I saw her petite nose, her lightly tanned skin, her rich hazel-green eyes glistening like emeralds, the same color of the forest leaves that she loved so deeply. A piece of my heart contracted. My breath was shallow, barely moving at all in my chest.

Ally and I were six years apart in age. A free-spirited and highly compassionate twenty-year-old, she had always demonstrated deep wisdom beyond her youthful age. Although I was the older sister, I often relied upon her support by tapping into her grounded perspective throughout our childhood years.

Almost immediately a memory of an exchange we'd had months prior flashed through my mind. I was having a difficult day at work, attempting to complete progress notes at the psychiatric center where I was employed. Fat tears ran like pearls down my cheeks, landing on the desk around me. I had grabbed my phone and proceeded to contact my sister, the one person in the world

I could trust with absolutely anything. She was in New Zealand, thousands of miles away, yet our connection could not have been deeper.

"Ally," I said to her, "I'm having such a hard day. I wish you were here." Out of the two of us, I had always been the sensitive, emotional one, like delicate wildflowers blowing in the wind. Ally was the earthly soil that lovingly cradled those wildflowers, giving them substance and shelter.

Her response was immediate and poignant: "It's going to be okay, Sissy. You're the strongest person I know, so just keep trucking along."

Those words echoed in my mind now, but they could not suffice to fill the void that was growing inside my chest minute by minute. I did not feel strong. I felt the opposite of strong—broken, lost, and scared. Where was my sister now, to capture those wildflowers that were scattered in that unforgiving wind?

Those wildflowers of mine were scattered for quite some time, as the next six days and nights unfolded and proceeded to hand our family the most horrific experience of our lives. My parents had received a phone call informing them that Ally was missing. Immediately, my father decided to fly to New Zealand and join the search party with my uncle, despite my mother's stubborn protests that everything was fine and she had probably just fallen somewhere and broken a leg.

The tricks that the mind plays to protect itself are impressive, as anyone who has ever endured great trauma can attest. Denial is like a cloak that we wrap around ourselves to protect our fragile bodies from the ferocity of the storm when it is simply too much to endure.

I wore that cloak of denial for the first several days of my sister's absence. It was a cloak I wore faithfully, repeatedly insisting without a doubt that she was alive, that the search party would find her intact—perhaps with an injury and some bruises inflicted by the mountainside, but otherwise completely well. When resignation began to creep into the voices of my family members, particularly once we received news from the search party that her backpack had been found—but not Ally—I clung onto that cloak of denial even more tightly.

On the Saturday night that they found her, my cousins and I were on a hike in one of Akron's many metroparks. Being nestled among the canopy of trees was the only slice of sanity I could cling onto in a world whose grounding had suddenly crumbled beneath my feet.

I was the one to spot it first—a massive tree with a thick, dense trunk that stood slightly separated from the others. It seemed to call out to me, and as I walked toward it, my heart stopped. Carved in huge letters on the tree trunk was the inscription "A. W."—my sister's initials. Chills radiated through my body, and my hair stood on end.

My mind raced back and landed on a particular conversation Ally and I had exchanged only months before, in which she had described to me the next tattoo she wanted: tree rings with a fingerprint in the middle. She wanted it in watercolor style on her ribs, she said, and she was sure that "Mom and Dad will hate it." She further explained the symbolism of the tattoo to me via text: "I've always loved trees because the rings build off each other; each one strengthens the tree. Each time you meet a person, you leave a mark on them, like a fingerprint. We have a responsibility to leave only good marks, leave good impressions, and consciously put positive energy into the world." Her words were moving and resonated deeply with me; however, at the time, little did either of us know how iconic those words would become.

Nearly three months later, those same words reverberated inside my head as I stared at the colossal tree in front of me. My sister, forever a lover of trees, had sent us a clear message from the other side.

Bits and pieces of the story began to coalesce, like tiny particles in a kaleidoscope. Ally, who had left to hike New Zealand's

Gillespie Pass at Mount Aspiring National Park, had become separated from the other hikers in her group during a storm. Visibility was low, they said, and she had taken a fall. They found her in the Young River, immersed in the water.

How fitting, I thought to myself in my numbed state. Water—the elixir of life, the eternal flow from which all things fall away and return. Water, with its fluid movement, is always in accord with the great harmony of life.

Forever an adventurer and committed to greeting each new experience on her trip with a firm and resolute "yes," Ally had embarked upon the hike despite the treacherous weather conditions. The scenery that she so deeply loved, the tremendous mountains and winding rivers and valleys of which she was so much a part, had beckoned my sister back to her everlasting home.

Ally's Life and LLA

Her passing created a massive impact, not only in our hometown of Akron, Ohio, but all around the world. For several months my family was bombarded with a plethora of letters, cards, and condolences from Ally's friends all around the globe. In her brief twenty years on this planet, Ally had traveled to New Zealand, Costa Rica, Israel, Guatemala, Malawi, and Tanzania. Much of her work had been conducted on service trips. Wherever she was in the world, Ally demonstrated a fierce desire to make the world a better place.

Her friends and family spoke with admiration about the same things: her zest and joy for life; her passion about helping the environment and preserving animal rights; her dedication to serving underprivileged populations, including the prison population and other disenfranchised groups. Her commitment to living her life fully, as well as her humility and sense of compassion for living things, was commonly noted. Listening to people speak about her, it was often difficult to believe that the person they were describing was my sister, let alone a twenty-year-old junior in college.

There is tremendous energy inherent in grief, and when that

energy can be constructively channeled somewhere, it can facilitate the healing process. This process happened quite organically within my family after we received a letter and picture from one of Ally's friends in New Zealand, Max Strotbeck. In his letter, Max explained how he had felt compelled to contribute to the search for Ally but had been informed that the search and rescue team was not accepting volunteers due to dangerous conditions. Determined to contribute in some way and to overcome his feeling of helplessness, Max created a banner that read For Ally and set out to climb the Single Cone mountain in Queenstown, New Zealand. He posted a picture of himself online that read: "Explore, climb, hike, and live like Ally. Seize the day and the remarkable moments it brings, and always live in the present. Carpe diem."

The words "Live Like Ally" quoted in this touching tribute spread like wildfire. Soon the phrase caught on not only with my parents but within our circle of family and friends as well. The phrase, abbreviated LLA, inspired us to greet the enormity of our loss. Like a compass, it guided us as to how Ally had lived her own life and how she would want us to receive our own pain—not with bitterness but with acceptance, love, and gratitude for the time our precious angel was here on Earth. Ally captured the essence of this viewpoint beautifully in her own words, in an essay she wrote after completing her first great walk, the Kepler Track in New Zealand: "In that moment, I understood that while situations may be beyond our control, we have responsibility in choosing our mind-set."

And choose our mind-set we did. In the midst of the rawest grief life had thrown our way, my family resolved to create a foundation to honor and continue my sister's legacy in the world. Thus the Live Like Ally Foundation was born, a foundation created with the intention of cultivating a commitment to the Earth, to humanity, and to all living things by focusing on environmental sustainability and providing financial support to young adults in achieving their own dreams and unique visions of making the world a better place.

The foundation specifically focused on taking action to improve environmental sustainability and food insecurity, issues which Ally was deeply passionate about.

While just a dream at first, and with no guarantee that anything substantial would come of it, my parents decided nonetheless to move forward with their vision. In a relatively short period of time, several applicants had applied and were accepted into LLA. The movement continued to gain momentum, sending young adults—"Ally's Allies"—to places all over the world, including Haiti, Peru, the Dominican Republic, Thailand, New Delhi, Ghana, and Spain. Gradually, a living legacy was born.

Twin Flames

Despite the goodness and hope that the LLA Foundation provided, even the creation of such a beautiful organization could not negate the deep pain of loss. Ally's passing plunged our family into a cavern of darkness. As I explained to a family friend, "When Ally fell into the river, the three of us fell with her."

Ally and I had the privilege of growing up in an extremely close family. It was not out of the ordinary for our second cousins, grandparents, and aunts and uncles to stop by for dinner or attend other family events. Our family support was extensive, and after Ally's passing, I would often reflect on this with gratitude and surmise that perhaps such extensive family support had been in place for a reason, like a giant support net to catch us as we took the fall.

Notably, Ally and I had grown close over the past several years. She was always my adoring little sister who followed me wherever I went, but it wasn't until the age gap between us began to close that we started to communicate and relate to each other on a deeper level. Once Ally went to college, our conversations began to expand and shift to more mature topics, including relationships with peers, intimate relationships, spirituality, and other worldly concerns.

Even amid her peers in college, she had always stuck out. She confessed to me once in a phone conversation how she felt different from other kids. She craved a more meaningful connection, deeper conversations about real topics that mattered—not, as she put it, "always just talking about partying or boys." Even as a nineteen-year-old, her depth and wisdom transcended that of her peer group. Undoubtedly, her concern for the world and other people had been her primary focus throughout her life.

She was my companion, my best friend, my confidant. Although I was blessed with close friends of my own who certainly played a priceless role in my healing process, there was no one in the entire world like my sister. I was left with an aching hole inside of me, a bottomless pit that no person or thing could ever fill.

When I was young, my mother used to remind us to cherish our sisterly bond. "Honey," she said, "Remember this. She is the only person in the world who has half of your DNA. She's the closest living thing that you have in this world."

My heart was broken. I called out for her in my sleep, and at night I woke up with tears streaming down my cheeks. In my dreams she would appear again, as if the accident had never happened, and I would awaken, only to remember the horrible truth of her death. During the day I replayed the sound of her voice in my head, saw her smiling face in my mind, heard the sound of her laughter like bells chiming in the wind. I yearned to embrace her in my arms, the way I used to when we were young.

The grief hit me with the ferocity of a freight train. Some days it took every ounce of energy I had to get out of bed in the morning. A tangible heaviness entered my body, weighing me down. My tears were endless, like rivers that never dried up. I simply could not imagine how I could continue for the rest of my life without my sister by my side. Nor did I want to continue. I felt like a wounded animal, hurting in a primal way that reached into the deepest caverns of my being. The pain transcended words.

My mind yearned to turn back time. Over and over I asked myself, "Why did this happen?" In its attempt to make sense of the insensible, and perhaps to instill a sense of control in a situation where I felt completely powerless, my mind created "what if" scenarios in which I played out different situations of that fateful day, each situation ending differently than what had actually happened: "What if she had decided not to go on the hike...what if she had stayed behind with her friends...what if I had visited her in New Zealand...what if..." My mind was relentless in its mission to rewrite history, to find some loophole that had been overlooked that would mean my beloved sister wasn't really gone. In the end, however, the story always brought me back to the same dreaded conclusion: Ally wasn't coming home, ever. With this realization, my grief knew no bounds.

It wasn't until many months later, when I was settled into a new life in a new city, that I fully understood the reason why the sense of loss within me was so profound.

The term "twin flames" entered my awareness for the first time while I was skimming through a book at a metaphysical expo. The words resonated with me for a reason I could not name; they conjured a memory deep within me, just beyond my conscious recollection. Little did I know that I had stumbled upon the keys to unlocking the mystery of my sister's passing, as well as my own life mission and purpose.

To date, there is a great deal of misinformation being circulated about twin flames—what they are and what purpose they serve. Twin flames are commonly thought to be romantically involved, and while that is certainly possible, it is not always the case. Actually twin flames can include any type of human relationship. Simply put, two people who are "twin flames" to one another are engaged in a deep type of soul relationship in which they have united for a common purpose that benefits themselves and all of humanity.

This is the case with me and Ally. Not only are the two of us connected as sisters, but we are connected as twin flames as well. Ally and I share the same soul, and prior to being born in this lifetime, the two of us mapped out our life mission and purpose, with full awareness that Ally's life would end at a young age. This is the only way that our work together in the world could be carried out—with Ally in the Spirit World and with me in the physical world, creating an energetic bridge between the realms. It was the only way our souls could complete the work we came here to do, which was to play a role in uplifting humanity's consciousness to its next stage of evolution.

My understanding of these truths continued to unfurl slowly, like a flower blooming open bit by bit. I was aided by many spiritual teachers, both on the Earth plane and beyond. Perhaps what served to convince me the most was not anything told to me by others but rather one of my memories from childhood:

From the time I was young, I was certain I was going to die young. A morbid thought, perhaps, but when I was a child, I didn't perceive it that way; it simply seemed like a fact. "I'm not going to have a very long life," I said to myself, as though I was reminding myself of something I had decided long ago. I felt this vague recollection on and off for the majority of my childhood, although I never spoke of it.

After my sister's death, I met with one of my spiritual teachers. I told her of this childhood recollection, and she said, "That was just a transference. You remembered that one of you was going to have a short life, but you thought it was you instead of your sister."

This remembrance of my and Ally's connection as twin flames, as well as her soul's intention to exit from this life at a young age, had existed inside my being from the time I was a young child. Indeed, I had always known that such a catastrophic event was going to happen, on some primordial level below my conscious awareness.

All of us have this vast reservoir of spiritual knowledge and recollection within us. We are born with our spiritual memories intact, but when the veil of the physical world descends, these recollections fade into the ocean of our unconscious mind, like a treasure chest that has sunk to the bottom of the sea. This treasure chest is not lost, however. There are methods of accessing that treasure again, such as through hypnosis, meditation, yoga, breath work, or other techniques that employ altered states of consciousness. Most often the journey we take to remembering such deep knowledge is a winding one that may span months or even years. Ironically, my own spiritual journey began several years before my sister died.

My Spiritual Awakening

As a child, I came into this world psychically open. I was hypersensitive to my surroundings, such as lights, sounds, and vibrations, and this sensitivity extended into the spiritual realm. Able to sense spirits and see energy at a young age, I found that this spiritual awareness was often misunderstood by adults around me. My various emotional fluctuations and intolerance to the harshness of the material world caused me to experience difficulty both in school and at home.

Efforts to treat and decrease this sensitivity, and therefore my suffering, led my parents to take me to doctors who all too readily labeled me with a misdiagnosis of childhood bipolar disorder. Doctors at that time had little understanding or appreciation for other factors that could contribute to the "symptoms" of hyperactivity and mood lability of a young child, especially factors that were not included in the most updated rendition of the Diagnostic and Statistical Manuel. Still to this day, there remains a large gap between the mental health field and the spiritual realm, and unfortunately this gap is too often overlooked and misunderstood. As a young nine-year-old girl in the 1990s, I paid a dear price for that gap.

This price had consequences that affected both my life and my family's lives for years. Piling on medication after medication to reduce the effects of my sensitivity, I became a walking zombie for most of my middle school and high school years, when my continued struggles eventually resulted in hospitalization and a full year in a residential treatment center at the age of seventeen. It wasn't until college—when I left home and had managed to wean off all my medications, as well as disregard the inaccurate diagnosis of bipolar disorder—that I at last began to lead what could be called a "normal" life.

However, the path for me was never normal, certainly not in the traditional sense of the word. At times I longed to feel more conventional and mainstream. Yet at my core, I always felt I was somehow different, although the words to explain this difference always eluded me. It was more of a felt sense and remembrance than it was a logical understanding. Other intuitives and empaths can surely relate to this feeling of being "different" from the norm.

I had shut down and effectively turned off my psychic sensitivities after I was misdiagnosed as a little girl, just as surely as a robber locking a safe full of money and disregarding the key. Having been made to feel there was something wrong with me for the majority of my childhood, I believed my sensitivity to be a problem and a burden. In fact I had managed to suppress my psychic gifts so much that my conscious mind had effectively forgotten that they existed at all. It wasn't until I completed my first yoga teacher training and adopted a formal daily meditation practice that these gifts began to rise to the surface of my consciousness again.

They revealed themselves gradually and gingerly, as if someone was shining the grime from a necklace of pearls, dusting them off one by one. I had forgotten how lustrous those pearls were. In fact, at first I felt a sense of fear and uncertainty in regard to my long-lost abilities. The same fears I experienced as a little girl rose to the surface yet again: I questioned my sanity, whether something was wrong with me, whether anyone in their right mind would ever understand me. I fervently sought out spiritual teachers and other like-minded individuals with whom I could share my experiences of the spiritual world.

Yet amid the haze of fear, there was a sense of deep joy contained within the experience. There was a feeling of empowerment and recognition in returning to the Spirit World, a world in which I had frolicked and explored and danced as a young child, a world I had thought I would never return to again. A sense of sweetness permeated within me as I closed my eyes to meditate and journey back into the place I had left behind long ago. It was a world of freedom, of love and light, a world where the sweetness of imagination and remembrance ruled, a world where the rigid boundaries of separation could not penetrate the constant flow of interconnectivity and oneness that was present everywhere.

The majority of my psychic awakening occurred in the form of visions, which I saw in my mind while meditating. Often these visions involved images of me undergoing initiations by stepping into a fire, symbolically representing the "burning up" of my old identity, my ego. In these visions I stepped forward not with fear but with willingness and acceptance. All the while I heard the voices of guides and angels in my mind. They greeted me with open arms and love as I experienced a blissful sort of welcoming back into the spiritual realms. Often I sensed the presence of other spiritual beings around me during the day. They revealed messages to me, such as the importance of cultivating trust, surrendering to the divine, and having faith, no matter what was presented to me upon my path.

Little did I know at the time that my guides on the other side were preparing me to withstand the trauma of my sister's death.

As I looked back after Ally's accident, all the puzzle pieces fell into place. It was like watching the outcome of a play from the end and seeing the bigger picture of why all the characters and events had unfolded exactly as they did. I understood that if I had not connected with the Spirit World again and received adequate preparation from my guides beforehand, I may not have been able to handle the magnitude of the loss from Ally's death. I may have succumbed to the grief and the overwhelming pain of loss, as I learned I had done in many of my past lives, thus creating a karmic pattern for myself to overcome in this lifetime. In fact, I saw that I had been given everything that I needed to absorb the shock of the trauma. My guides provided me with all the tools and knowledge that I so desperately needed to hold onto in those initial stages of grief, much like a drowning man clinging to a lifeboat amid a turbulent sea.

Through the event of my sister's death, spiritual awakening of the rawest kind was forced upon me. All that I had studied, mediated on, read about, and searched for in seminars, in books, and on my yoga mat was thrust upon me as powerfully as a lightning bolt striking down from the sky. Oftentimes on the spiritual path, we convince ourselves of how evolved we are, yet until we come face to face with the groundlessness of our lives and the deep wounds of the heart, we do not truly know what it feels like to step into the fire of spiritual transformation.

Once that fire is unleashed, there is only one way to respond: convert the flames into the alchemy that will lead to spiritual rebirth, or else perish.

Integration of Spirit and Form

It was a long process of recovery and healing, one that is still ongoing to this day. Anyone who has endured loss and stepped into their own spiritual fire knows that there is never a time when the pain goes away and when the healing is "complete." The process of healing is subtle and refined in nature. It is not so much that the pain goes away; rather, it gradually morphs into something less heavy and more manageable. A person's relationship to the pain changes until its presence becomes less alarming and more familiar, less of a conflict and more of an accepted guest in the home.

For me, one of the most difficult aspects of healing was reconciling the gap between the pain I felt in my ego and the inner knowing of my spirit. As a spiritual seeker with psychic abilities, I thought of myself as someone with a relatively significant amount of spiritual awareness. In other words, studying yoga, meditation, Reiki, psychology, counseling, and the healing arts, I felt as though I had developed a high level of understanding about topics pertaining to life after death. After all, I communicated with my spirit guides and deceased loved ones! I was no stranger to the higher etheric realms; actually, I was a well-traveled guest. I had an intellectual understanding of the eternal nature of the soul. I had an established meditation practice and was under the guidance of spiritual teachers in my community.

Yet—for all of this guidance and experience—the horror I felt at the loss of my sister was devastatingly real. I had knowledge of the illusion, yet I still felt the ground cracking open beneath me. I understood the eternal nature of the soul, yet the sense of loss I felt was as deep and vast as the ocean. I understood the cycle of grief— I had actually studied it in my graduate school curriculum—yet I still found myself completely bombarded by the intensity and confusion of my emotions. I knew the symptoms and signs of trauma from reading textbooks and working with multiple traumatized clients, yet I still felt surprised when I witnessed myself observing the very signs I had read about. I understood that even though my sister's death was an accident, on a soul level, it was her choice and her own creation. I knew she had chosen that particular path for herself, yet I still was flabbergasted by the senselessness of it all.

What's more, I had the ability to connect instantly with my sister in the Spirit World. Because of my sensitivity, I was able to feel her. Not only did I hear her voice in my head, but I also saw her and felt her presence with me. I conveyed messages from her to the people she cared about, including my parents and her friends. I heard her reassurance and affirmations of love and comfort in my head on a daily basis: "I'm here with you, Sissy. I'll never leave you. Our relationship is just different now. We can talk anytime you want."

These messages comforted me deeply, and I treasured them as a gift. Never had I cherished my psychic sensitivity like I did in the months following my sister's death. Certainly such messages are more than most grieving family members receive. Most mourners would give anything just to hear their loved one's voice again, and here I was, communicating with my sister and feeling her presence all the time. It was a blessing of the highest kind.

Yet it brought challenges too. Why couldn't I reconcile my knowledge and visceral experience of the Spirit World with my sense of grief? Why did I sense this division between the truths that my own spirit knew and my feelings of loss and rage? It was as if I sensed two different personalities within me, that of my grief-tormented small self and that of my expansive, eternal self. The wider understanding of my higher self was completely inaccessible to that of my small self, although cognitively my ego understood everything on an intellectual level. The gap seemed to be insurmountable.

To make matters worse, my knowledge of the Spirit World caused me to feel guilty for experiencing grief at such a profound level. "I shouldn't be feeling this way," I said to myself. "I know better than this!" Grief is grief, though, and ultimately it must be honored and allowed. Grief is one of the most profound experiences we as human beings can go through, and it has many lessons to impart to us. I learned that there is no room for judgments, timetables, or expectations when it comes to working through grief.

In the beginning of my grieving process, I tried to escape the intensity of my emotions by dwelling in the etheric realms of reality. I meditated and devoured all the books, information, and workshops I could find on mediumship and how to connect with spirit. To the best of my ability, I dwelled in the place where my sister was, either through meditating or connecting my energy with hers. Through her transition, the portal had opened for me, and I could access the world of light and bliss that she was in. She was my one-way ticket to the Spirit World, and I didn't want to return.

But eventually I always did. No matter how much knowledge or understanding I attained in the Spirit World, at the end of the day, I was still confined to my human body. I could learn and master all the tricks in the world—astral projection, meditation, hypnosis, altered states of consciousness—yet eventually I always had to come back into my body and my ego. And therefore, of course, to the pain.

So there I was in the first several months after the death of my sister, engaged in a dance in which I energetically whirled back and forth between spirit and form: between my higher self—which was full of infinite knowing, clarity, and perfect understanding— and my ego, which was full of pain, rage, and a deep sense of loss. When I wasn't dwelling in my spirit, I was back in form, meaning my ego. The pain of returning back to the grief was indescribable.

The problem, I came to realize, was that there was no middle ground. I was either dwelling only in the Spirit World or only in the physical world; there was no integration of the two. Herein was my conundrum. I couldn't stay in either realm, and eventually I returned to the opposite place of where I'd been. I couldn't dwell in the Spirit World indefinitely, because I had a physical body as well as responsibilities and relationships on the Earth plane. Conversely, I couldn't dwell permanently on the Earth plane, because my spirit longed for the connection and clarity of Source. I was like a Ping-Pong ball being bounced back and forth in a never-ending match with no real winner. In other words, it was a catch-22.

Forgetfulness of Being and the Ascension of Consciousness
Although my dilemma was an internal one, it served as a mirror that reflected back the same sense of fragmentation in the collective consciousness and in the world. I realized I wasn't the only one experiencing difficulty in finding the balancing point between the two realms. In fact, the more I progressed on my spiritual journey in the months following Ally's passing, the more I came to realize the dire state of our world.

Human beings are here to integrate the body and the spirit, the physical and the spiritual. We cannot dwell in one and forget the other because both are crucial elements of who we are. In actuality there is no separation between the spiritual realm and the physical; they are one, both different extensions of Source expressing itself. Learning to live in the physical world with a remembrance of our true nature as spirit is called enlightenment. It is in this state of awareness that our true creative power lies.

Yet we cannot ever access this integrated point without reclaiming that which we have forgotten, which is our identity as divine souls. This remembrance of our true identity cannot be attained through the ordinary conscious mind; it can only be *sensed* through being.

In this context, "being" refers to the part of you that is not defined by any of the roles you play or by anything you say or do. "Being" refers to the unlimited consciousness that you are. It is the eternal aspect of you that was present before you came into this life and will continue to be present after you die. "Being" is the silence, the spaciousness, and the container in which your soul resides.

As a culture and as a whole, we have forgotten our true nature in being. We have come to identify solely with our identity in ego, which is based upon labels such as "mother," "father," "coworker," "business owner," and "friend," yet none of these labels can come even close to containing our true vastness. Our entire identity structure is based upon the illusionary belief that our consciousness ceases to exist beyond the walls of the physical body. In this belief we are sadly mistaken, and we are also missing the entire point of our existence.

Forgetfulness of our true nature has been progressing for many centuries and is now reaching a tipping point. This forgetfulness comes with a high price that compromises the security, stability, and well-being of ourselves and of the Earth. In forgetting our true nature as spirit, we also forget our connection to one another and to the planet. We forget the sacred interconnectedness of life. This ancient wisdom was known for millennia by the aboriginal people of the Earth, when the balance was in harmony before the advancement of technology. Slowly but surely, such ancient truths were tossed to the side in favor of the rise of capitalism and mental attitudes that favored success and money over virtually all else.

This is the cycle that humanity has created for itself. We have gotten ourselves tied into a giant knot, and it will take the effort and intention of every human being to straighten it out. If we do not "untie the knot," so to speak, the survival of all of humankind is at stake. You only need to turn on the television to see the multitude of problems facing humanity, such as starvation, lack of clean water and resources, violence, genocide, mass shootings, diseases, and terrorist attacks to predict the trajectory of mankind's path should some massive change in our mind-set not occur.

It is not as bleak a situation as it may seem, though. Although the consequences are very real, and an understanding of the seriousness of the consequences is important, it is equally important to recognize the power that mankind has to shift the current state of the world.

Each human being is incredibly and vastly powerful. This power is sourced not from a person's ego, or from any material or monetary success that a person has achieved, but rather from the light of a person's soul, which is a powerhouse of knowledge and creativity. This power is magnified thousand-fold when a person lives in conscious awareness of their true identity as a divine being. A person who has reclaimed their identity in being is a person who will consistently act in accordance with their spirit, which is always kind, loving, patient, generous, compassionate, and respectful. Coming back to our true nature is therefore synonymous with bringing these qualities into the world. Awakening to our true nature is the most important work that we can do for the salvation of ourselves and one another.

We can rest assured that this awakening is already beginning to happen, as a new age of awareness is taking root within our country and around the world. Mankind is expanding into its next stage of evolution, but it will not be a shift that occurs without pain and strife. To a large extent, the pain and suffering that we see in our world today is a reflection of this shift beginning to occur. Although it is not necessary for the shift in human evolution to cause resistance and pain, it will deliver that to those who are not properly prepared for the change. This is because the beliefs and infrastructure of the old paradigm of consciousness must collapse and give way to create space for the new paradigm of consciousness to take hold. Outdated and prejudiced religious beliefs, as well as limiting cultural beliefs and stereotypes, must fall to the wayside. Humanity can no longer afford to remain attached to these belief structures if we are to ascend to the new era. To those who lack understanding or recognition of this process, however, such changes can seem radical and have the potential to produce deep-seated, fear-based reactions.

In general, people are resistant and slow to accept change. The ego in particular prefers for things to stay at the status quo, because it derives its sense of security from feeling as though it understands the way things operate. Resisting the shift in humanity's evolution is futile, however; it is as futile as it is for a parent to fight against the natural growth of their young child into a preschooler. Humanity is the child, and it is fighting desperately to grow into a more expanded consciousness, one that is based on principles of love, unity, interconnection, and truth.

Collectively and individually, we are moving from a fear-based understanding of our world into a worldview of abundance and love. If we look around, we can see evidence of this shift happening constantly. Changes are being made both on the micro and the macro levels. The change that is occurring is inevitable; what is within each of our control is how we choose to respond to that change. We can decide to resist and fight against the shift of consciousness that is happening because it challenges our worldview and causes us to feel fearful, or we can decide to greet the changes with open arms, willing to assist one another the best we can, trusting that the final outcome of the shift will result in something more beautiful, pure, and whole than we could have ever imagined. It is the same choice I faced in confronting the death of my sister: I couldn't change the fact that she had died, but I could choose how I wanted to respond to the loss.

My own awakening process, ignited through the devastating the loss of my sister, eventually led me to reclaim my identity in being once again. It was Ally's journey to New Zealand that forged the path for me to take the most important journey of all: one of coming back home to myself.

Awareness of Being: The Journey Back to Yourself
Although I experienced significant spiritual growth in the weeks following Ally's death, it wasn't until months after she passed and I had settled into a new city that I experienced the profound awakening experience that transformed my entire life. It was from that experience that this book was born.

My awakening was initiated by my participation in a shamanic ceremony in which I ingested a traditional plant-based medicine called Ayahausca, known to Native people for hundreds of years and used for its healing properties. The outcome of this ceremony was one which I never could have predicted. It catapulted me on a journey deep into the realms of the Spirit World, the place I had so longed to return to, the place in which my sister dwelled.

The experience was at once both horrifying and wonderfully beautiful. I was back in the dream world, a world composed primarily of sensations, colors, shapes, and visions. The "me" whom I had constructed and the story of "Emily Willen" that I had so carefully woven together for the previous twenty-six years of my life on Earth was annihilated almost instantaneously. In other words, my ego completely dissolved, and I found myself once again back in that space of oneness that my soul so desperately yearned for.

The experience itself lasted for several hours, but in the space where I was, there was no time. I had slipped into a timeless dimension in which designations of minutes and hours were completely meaningless. There was only Now, and everything was contained within Now.

Throughout the duration of the ceremony, much knowledge was revealed to me—but not in the way we are familiar with, which is through the realm of the mind. The knowing came through the opening of my pineal gland as well as my third eye. It also came through the dissolution of my ego, which included the boundaries of the material world.

I saw everything there was to see because I *was* everything. I felt deep sorrow and pain, and I felt unconditional joy and love, and I understood them to be coexisting together, not as two separate emotional states but rather as two parts of the same whole. Likewise I was shown both the light, the pure brightness and white purity of Source, and the darkness, the deepest, rawest caverns of humanity's suffering and pain, which contained my own. There was no distinction between them. Rather, they coincided and linked together effortlessly, each feeding into the other.

I connected with Ally during the ceremony. The medicine I ingested lifted the veils that separated the physical world from the Spirit World, so I was able to connect with her effortlessly. I could hear and speak with her as clearly as I'd spoken with my mother on the phone earlier that day. We communicated not through verbal language but rather through telepathy.

With unparalleled and complete clarity, I understood and remembered everything I had always known. The searching was over. There was nothing to strive for, nothing to look for, nothing to do or become. I had returned to the space within myself, which I had never truly left.

The journey did nothing but take me back to myself. It was a journey that took me from the world of form back into the world of spirit, effectively flipping the role of my ego and my soul so that rather than seeing the world through the lens of my egoic mind, I saw everything through the lens of my eternal spirit. Within the domain of my spirit, there was no questioning, no seeking, and no judgment. There was simply pure consciousness and awareness.

Toward the end of the journey, I could feel the medicine wearing off, and I knew the experience was drawing to a close. I watched as the reality in front of me, or what I had perceived reality to be, shimmered back and forth in my vision like static on a television.

"No, no," I cried out loud, to no one really but myself. "I don't want to go back. Please don't make me go back!"

While pleading to stay in the Spirit World, through the process of grace, I was subsequently shown the magnificent gift of being born back into a physical body.

I became aware of a sensation of the deepest joy and love imaginable spreading through my body. I wasn't seeing anything in particular; rather, I was in a realm of pure sensation and experience, similar to that which children undergo before they are born into the world. I knew at once the glory of being gifted a human life, and I knew that the feeling of joy was what I had felt before I had been born into this life as Emily Willen. It was my soul's joy of journeying back again into physical existence.

In that moment, I watched as creation began to unfold before me. In a moment of instant recognition, I saw the creative Source begin to bring me and the universe into being, motivated solely out of divine love. I watched as the world in all of its myriad shapes and forms manifested. I saw people of all backgrounds and histories coming into the world. I saw, or rather sensed, animals of all species and plant life and the vast interconnectedness of the world come into play. I saw the Earth and all of its creations being born, and I was one of them. In that moment, I was face to face with the creative Source of the universe. It was the Source of all religions, all worlds, and all life. The sheer power of it coursed through my entire body like electric voltage.

"God!" I cried out, because it was the only syllable I could possibly utter.

As soon as I said the word, I understood it to be the *Word*. I understood viscerally what God was, not with my mind but through my third eye and heart. Through transcending the limitations of my ego, I caught a brief glimpse of the infinity, the primal power, the Source engine of the entire universe, which in our language we feebly define as "God." In truth, that Source is infinitely more vast than we could ever understand. In a heartbeat I knew and understood that all religions were representations of this one Source, which, if broken down into one singular feeling state, could be recognized simply as loving awareness.

And so I was reborn back into the world and into my body once again, yet I was never the same thereafter. The experience had shifted the molecules within my bones. Nothing I looked at was the same, yet it was no different than it had always been; I was simply awake and able to see.

For months after this spiritual experience, I dwelled in the vibration of pure joy. There was no resistance to be found anywhere in my body or my mind. I was content to merely sit and be. Retreating deeply into myself, I rested at home in the heart of my being. My relationships with others were more wholesome and pure, for I had no sense of egoic attachment or agendas from which to operate. My understanding of my own place in the universe, as well as my connection to my soul, was constant and never ending. My sense of time dissolved each day, until—rather than adhering strictly to a linear sense of seconds, minutes, and hours—all of my experiences effortlessly fused together into one continuous flow. I was the most content and joyful I had ever been in my life, but the sense of deep serenity did not come from anything external happening around me. Rather, it radiated out from within me. At last I had found and opened that treasure chest that resided at the core of my being.

Yet as the months piled on and life began to resume its natural rhythm, this spiritual experience became less paramount in my consciousness as I gravitated toward more responsibilities and commitments within the external world. Despite all of our good intentions and practices, the ego remains a slippery and resilient creation with its own agenda and way of functioning. As many spiritual awakenings as we may have in which we transcend the ego, it will nonetheless try its best to reestablish its grip on our perception of the world around us.

Recognizing this process occurring within me, I realized that once again I was polarizing between the worlds of spirit and form. It wasn't until I had a discussion with a friend that I realized the necessity of creating a new mode of being that integrated the experience of both spirit and form: awareness of being. For I wasn't in the same state of consciousness I had been in prior to the ceremony; indeed, the shift in my consciousness had been so profound that I would never be able to return to that state again. Yet as the months progressed and that heightened spiritual state lessened, I also didn't remain in the clarity that had been accessible to me during the ceremony. I needed to create a new way of being that integrated both perceptual experiences. Thus, the concept of awareness of being was born.

A System of Healing, Integration, and Awakening

Awareness of being was the key concept I had been searching for. It was the middle point that united my experience in the physical world with my understanding of the spiritual world. It was the answer to resolving the polarization both within my psyche and within the psyche of the collective consciousness. It was the "golden ticket," so to speak, that humanity had been missing.

The creation of this healing system unfurled for me simultaneously with understandings from my spiritual awakening. I came to understand that it was part of my and Ally's destiny as twin souls to work together between the realms to create this healing system. Actually, Ally could help me infinitely more with the creation of the system in her nonphysical form—and that is precisely what she did.

Awareness of being is a system of healing, integration, and awakening. Although the system is multifaceted in its approach, ultimately it has a single intention: to awaken you to your true nature as Creator, thereby aligning you with the energy of Source so you are free to manifest the life of your dreams here on Earth. In doing so, you effectively merge spirit with form and are free to embody your divine purpose in the world.

In this new era of consciousness, the world needs people who embody their divine creative power. Rather than diminishing anyone else's success, one person's ability to thrive is representative of us all. One person's success propels all of humanity forward. It is imperative that we learn to uplift ourselves and one another.

Awareness of being is a system to do just that. This knowledge is not necessarily anything new; rather, it is a system that has taken ancient knowledge and organized it in a novel way. Each part of the system works together and feeds into the others. Rather than a linear approach, it is circular in nature.

There are three components in this system. The first component is largely related to the content that has been discussed here, which is bridging the gap between the ego and the spirit. Many of us spend our entire lives dwelling in one realm or the other—either we exist primarily in the physical world, with virtually no connection to our spirit, or we dwell primarily in the etheric realms and experience difficulty creating tangible results in the physical world. In order to thrive in this new age and embody our divine purpose on Earth, we must learn to integrate the two realms. The first part of the healing system, detailed in this book, assists you in bridging the gap between ego and spirit.

The second part of this healing system is a result of the work done in the first part. Integrating your spirit and ego leads you to awareness of being. Only when you find this middle ground can you reach awareness of being. Think about it—if you're not only dwelling in your spirit and you're not only dwelling in your ego, where are you? You're in the space between the two. This is the space we call *beingness*, the space in which your soul resides, and it is this essential *beingness* that our world has forgotten. In order to heal ourselves, we must retrieve this fundamental awareness of our being. It may be called awakening, or enlightenment, or any other term, but essentially it is the ability to recognize ourselves as divine and to live in awareness of our true nature as Creators. We are not separate from the Creator and from creation but rather are one with it.

From the understanding that arises from awareness of being comes the third and final part of the healing system, which involves claiming your creative power and manifesting the life of your dreams. Only when you recognize and know on a visceral level your identity as a divine being can you manifest your true purpose in the world. The manifestation of your dreams is meant to be easy. It is not supposed to be a struggle. You were born into this life and this body in absolute, unbridled joy. Before you incarnated, you had clear knowledge of the journey you were to embark upon, and you knew you had everything you needed to succeed. In reclaiming this knowledge, you reclaim your power. You are infinitely powerful beyond measure and contain everything you need within you to create the life that you desire. The three components of this system are meant to guide you in returning back to your true self so that you may create harmony within your own spirit and also within the world.

This book will highlight the first component of the system, which is the integration of spirit and form. In the first part of this book, titled "Purandev Speaks," I highlight spiritual lessons about living in the physical realm. In the second half of the book, Ally provides valuable information about the Spirit World. She gives us important knowledge, not only about the process of acclimation and learning that takes place on the other side after death but also about lessons that souls study in their continued education as spirits. The third part of this book then brings everything full circle by focusing on the concept of awareness of being, which allows us to unite the polarities so that we may return, both in ourselves and in our world, to that place of oneness that transcends duality.

Support Beyond this Book: Applying
Awareness of Being into your Life
As time progressed I began to realize the profound implications of this healing system. Awareness of being was a beautiful gift given

by Source that had the power to restore humanity to its essential nature. It was not something that could be grasped by the mind, but rather asked to be cultivated through the heart. It was not something that needed to be taught, but rather requested the time, care, and attention to naturally blossom forth from within.

Inspired by the power of this healing consciousness in my own life, I designed a 6 week Masterclass called Surrender into Being. The intention of this Masterclass is to provide clear, structured support for people who are called to deepen their understanding of the state of consciousness called 'awareness of being' that is explored in this book and to practice applying it within the container of their daily lives.

The Surrender into Being Masterclass is designed to support your consciousness in returning to the fundamental state of your inner beingness. Each module within the class contains information about various spiritual lessons. Each module also provides a practical exercise designed to support you in applying the information. Taken together, the modules are complete lessons in themselves, yet they also work interdependently with one another. Every module in the class is like one side of a diamond, each of which serves to bring you back to your true essence, the space between your spirit and your ego—awareness of being.

Through my journey of maneuvering the many layers of grief following Ally's passing, I was also inspired to create a conscious community platform called Ally & Me. The intention of this platform was two-fold: first, to provide a safe and sacred space for people to honor those whom they have lost and second, to provide a container for the exploration and discussion of topics pertaining to the afterlife. I felt in my heart that both aspects of what this social platform provided were vitally important to the expansion of the collective consciousness.

Indeed, after her passing Ally appeared to me numerous times, emphasizing and confirming the importance of removing the fear, confusion, and stigma surrounding the topic of death. She told me it was so important that people know the truth: that there is nothing to fear about the transition we call death; that our souls are supported by ever-present and loving beings who guide us on our journey back to the Spirit World; and that our souls are eternal, meaning that we never truly die.

It is my prayer that these offerings serve to provide containers for people to heal their hearts from the experience of grief and the fear of death, as well as access the profound state of peace that arises from living in communion with their own being. To find out more about these offerings and platforms, please visit my website at www.purandevkaur.com.

In Conclusion: When She Fell, She Flew

For months and even years after Ally passed, my mother was haunted by nightmares of the suffering that she imagined my sister may have felt in the stark and rugged New Zealand landscape. *Was she in pain,* she asked herself, *was she scared, or cold, or lonely in those final moments?* These heart-wrenching questions were asked during sleepless nights with the tenderness and grief that only a mother's heart could contain. I offered my mother as much comfort as I could during those agonizing moments, hugging and assuring her that God had protected our beloved girl—yet still harboring those same questions within the deepest caverns of my own heart.

Ultimately it wasn't me that provided my mother with the assurance of Ally's easeful departure, but Ally herself. Countless times after her death, Ally appeared to me and repeatedly assured me that she had not suffered, that her death was not prolonged, but rather that it had happened so quickly and instantaneously that it had taken her soul some time to actually process what had happened. "Tell mom I'm okay, Sissy," she had told me. "Tell her I wasn't in any pain." Ally wanted, more than anything, to give my mother that message. She wanted my mother to receive that knowing and have peace of mind, for she knew that my mother's pain was fueled by the thought of Ally having suffered.

I did relay that message to my mother in the hopes that it would assuage the wound in her heart. Now, just as Ally wanted me to relay a message to my mother, she wants me to relay a message to you as well. Her message—which is the essence of this book—is applicable and accessible, and holds powerful implications for us all. The message is this:

> There is nothing to fear about life or death.
> You can never truly die.
> You are an infinite creator having a brief human experience to learn soul lessons for your highest growth.
> There is an intelligent, conscious, loving source guiding every aspect of your life.
> The learning never stops.
> You can never truly fall.
> You are indescribably loved.

Contrary to my mom's deepest fears, when Ally transitioned from this world, she did not fall off the New Zealand mountainside—she flew. Which is to say, she reached completion in her human journey and answered with a firm "yes" to the next part of her spiritual evolution. She now lovingly offers you, the reader, messages of spiritual truth to serve as beacons of wisdom to light the way for your journey.

Through reading this book, you, like Ally and me, will be taken on a journey. It is like the journey that our souls undertake from the day we are born until the day we return back to the Spirit World, the place from which we came. It is the journey of coming into form from spirit and leaving form to return to spirit again. It is the journey of forgetting your true nature and of rediscovering, through awareness of being, that what you were searching for was ultimately inside of you all along.

PART ONE: SPIRIT
PURANDEV SPEAKS

THE JOURNEY IN

You are about to embark upon a journey.

It is a journey you have taken many times before, though
you do not consciously remember that this is so.

It is a journey of great wonder and beauty, and your being
feels only the deepest joy at the thought of returning to this
place called Earth, where you know you will experience grand
adventures. There will be sorrows, too, of course, just as you
planned, yet they are part of the journey as well. Together
all of the pieces create a tapestry, a kaleidoscope of different
experiences, each one a small reflection of the larger whole.

Everything you need is contained within you. You are a universe
unto yourself. You lack nothing and contain all. You will forget
this knowledge, of course, as the veil of illusion sets in once you
merge with your physical body—just as you knew you would—
and the uncoiling of this truth and remembrance is the entire
point. The remembrance is the journey.

And so you begin…

CHAPTER ONE

PEELING BACK THE VEIL OF ILLUSION

The "veil" refers to the boundary that separates the Earth plane from the Spirit World. This veil separates the two realms and keeps the energy of the Earth plane distinct. Throughout history, many ancient cultures were aware of this veil and defined it with different names, using various practices to transcend and journey beyond it. In Hinduism the veil is known as maya (illusion), and it was taught that through meditation, a person could learn to see beyond the illusion of the physical world. Indigenous practices have employed other methods to journey beyond the veil, such as shamanic journeying and vision quests. Despite differences in how the veil was defined and understood, however, the reason in journeying beyond it remained the same: to transcend duality and unite the two realms, thereby bringing the truth and knowledge from the Spirit World onto the Earth for purposes of healing and enlightenment.

With the advent of technology and rapid advances in communication in recent decades, however, the ancient ways of journeying beyond the veil were largely discarded. Valuable wisdom that was used for centuries by our ancestors was tossed aside. Humanity effectively lost itself in its own dream. We became the dream, so to speak, and forgot that we were the dreamers. In other words, humanity lost itself in the illusion of the outer world.

However, as humankind progresses and ascends to greater levels of consciousness, the veil is beginning to thin and become accessible again. A resurgence of the ancient wisdom that once was second nature to our ancestors is returning to our world. Collectively, humanity's connection to the spiritual world is becoming stronger. More people are experiencing spiritual awakenings, and more still are becoming seekers of spiritual truth, wisdom, and knowledge. In other words, a renaissance of consciousness is occurring throughout the world at an unprecedented rate. Is the veil becoming thinner because of the increased consciousness permeating our world, or is our increased consciousness what is causing the veil to thin? In all likelihood the two phenomena affect one another, creating a feedback loop of sorts. In any case, the result remains the same: the veil between the worlds becomes more transparent every day, allowing us not only to access higher spiritual states of consciousness but also to make greater contact with beings in the spiritual realms.

With this thinning of the veil, spiritual truth and wisdom can more easily spill into the physical realm and filter into the collective consciousness of humanity. As a result, one of the most important spiritual truths that people are waking up to today is the realization that the world around us is nothing more than a holographic illusion. That is to say, the physical world that you glimpse with your two eyes is not the "true" reality. You may think of it as being the dream, and you are the dreamer.

Everyone and everything that you experience around you is part of a stage setup for your soul's evolution and growth. The world that you see with your physical eyes is like God's playground for humankind, a space for human beings to enact and clear their karmas, to learn their lessons, to love, to search, to connect, and to find their way back once again to their true, divine nature—as long as that process may take. In this sense, the world is a beautiful gift from the Creator, yet it is not the true reality.

You can sense this truth for yourself by looking around and realizing that the tangible world that you see is transitory. Everything in your experience, from your physical body to the weather outside to the building you work in to the car you drive, will eventually meet its end. Everything in the world is constantly changing. It is like a continuous dance, a never-ending flow as old as time itself, in which the winds of change permeate the cosmos. Pause and ask yourself for a moment: What in your life is *not* subject to change? What in the world around you would be exactly the same if you traveled forward in time five hundred years from now? No matter who you are or what kind of lifestyle you are living, your answer would be the same: nothing. Nothing would be the same because everything in the tangible world is subject to change. The only things that would remain the same are the things that are part of the intangible world of being, such as a deep sense of presence and love. These qualities, which are ultimately one and the same, are eternal and are therefore more "real" than the physical world that you glimpse around you in your daily life.

If we define what is "real" around us simply by what we can see through our physical sensory system, then we are making a grave mistake. There exists a deeper reality beneath the one we can see with our physical eyes, and it is from this deeper reality that the physical world around us was born. We, too, were born from this unseen reality, and although we may have forgotten its existence, that does not mean that it is no longer there or that we are not intimately connected to it.

What is truly "real," therefore, cannot be defined through the physical senses alone. Looking deeper, we can see that our definition of reality is nothing more than a set of agreed-upon assumptions that have been culturally handed down from one generation to the next without question, something that may be called "culturally agreed-upon reality." Try asking yourself why you do any sort of traditional activity, such as going to church or eating a turkey at Thanksgiving dinner. Probe deeper and you will find the answer is because you were taught that it was "right" to do so. Your family taught you because their family taught them, and so on, until it became a mutually agreed-upon "truth." It became accepted as truth, yet when we are brave enough to peel back the veil and to see beyond it, we realize that many of our culturally agreed-upon truths are completely arbitrary.

Why might humanity do this? Why do we create such elaborate agreed-upon rules and conditions, which we pass down from generation to generation, even when they are disempowering and stifling to the growth of our consciousness? Why do we reject the notion of a deeper reality that transcends the one we see with our physical eyes? Why are we so reluctant to pull back the layer of that evanescent veil that surrounds us and to peek at what lies beyond it?

We create rules and conditions because they make us feel safe. Actually, what it is really doing is making the ego feel safe. To the ego, there is nothing scarier than beginning to peek beyond the veil, because it threatens its entire basis of reality, as well as its existence.

Ego is the part of your personality that is identified with your story: who you are, where you were born, what you do for a living. The ego's entire identity structure is dependent upon the physical world. That is why questioning some of humanity's most deeply held beliefs and traditions is so uncomfortable and threatening to the ego. Attachment to the physical world is the ego's primary Source of existence, so to realize that the world you perceive around you is nothing more than a collective dream drastically threatens the ego's sense of survival.

For example, if you have ever experienced a huge change in your life that disrupted your sense of identity, such as a divorce, the loss of a loved one, or the loss of a job, you may have experienced feelings of fear, pain, and discomfort that were tied to the situation. These feelings occurred within you because the ego was reacting fearfully to such change. If the ego can't grasp onto things to identify itself with, such as a particular occupation or relationship role, then it starts to fall into the stickiness of ambiguity that underlies all of existence.

More than anything, the ego wants to feel safe. It wants to feel secure, and it finds that sense of security by attaching to tangible things and circumstances around it: "As long as I still have this relationship, I'm okay. I have this job, and it gives me a good income, so I don't have to worry. I know what to expect every day at work, so nothing can hurt me." Such beliefs are likely to be subconscious, and a person may not even be aware that they are deriving their sense of security from the world around them; yet, until a person begins to become spiritually awakened, this is almost always the case.

The truth is that deriving a sense of security from the outside world is pointless. It is as pointless as trying to stop water from flowing downstream. As stated earlier, the outer world around you is constantly subject to change, and the more a person tries to resist that change, the more they will experience suffering. Resistance to change is always fear based, and in actuality there is nothing to fear. The more a person begins to derive their sense of security from their own inner world, from their own sense of beingness, the less fear they will experience within their life.

What is unchanging dwells within you. You are what is unchanging. The formless, intangible aspect of beingness and presence is one with who you are. The more you begin to acknowledge its existence inside of you and return to that place of beingness throughout your day, the more you will learn to release egoic fear and clinging.

Do not fight against the ego. Welcome it instead with open arms. If the egoic part of you is a stream, then the part of you that resides in beingness is an infinite ocean that can soothe the ego's fear and apprehension. Your ego is but a small aspect of your consciousness, and it represents only the tip of a very dense and large iceberg that reaches deep into the trenches of the sea. The strength of your being is vast and powerful beyond your wildest comprehension. Yet you cannot access that vastness by focusing only on the egoic state, which is ordinary waking consciousness.

How does one surpass the egoic state of the mind? It is a question that sages, yogis, and medicine men and women around the world have been posing for millennia. At the dawn of this new age, the answer is the same as it was hundreds of years ago. Our quest for understanding and answers has brought us on a journey back to the knowledge of our ancestors, and the answer is still this: we surpass the egoic state of mind by tapping into the power of the present moment.

The power of the present moment is that it annihilates your ego. Or, in other words, it destroys your story: the ego cannot survive in the present moment. It relies on a sense of past and future to define itself. That is why the ego clings and attaches itself so ferociously to thoughts of a past long gone or to thoughts of a potential future that hasn't even arrived yet. It yearns to dwell in those places because as long as it does so, it remains attached to the illusion of the past and the future and keeps them "alive" in the mind, so to speak; in other words, that attachment keeps the ego alive and functioning, and all of its neuroses along with it.

Thoughts of the past and the future feed the functioning of the ego. Because there is nothing more threatening to the ego than the present moment, it needs those thoughts in order to survive. In reality, however, the concept of time as we understand it is the greatest illusion of all. Think about it: How much of your daily waking reality is consumed and driven by thoughts of the past or propelled by thoughts of the future? Truthfully, what we collectively consider to be the past is nothing more than a constellation of old stories, definitions, and ideas that you have collected about yourself given the experiences in your life up until now. Many of those ideas, in fact, were not even created by you but rather were given to you by others through the process of indoctrination and social programming. Similarly, the notion of the future as we think of it is merely an imagined projection of the mind. We think of what could happen and sometimes act as if it has already happened. We can even work ourselves into heightened emotional states as a result of imagining a particular future outcome that hasn't actually occurred yet.

Neither past nor future is real, but the egoic mind needs to treat them as such. It depends upon their existence to sustain itself. Holding onto projections and attachments to the past and the future prevents the ego from having to glimpse beyond the veil to the true reality underneath. The ego actively avoids glimpsing beyond the veil because doing so would threaten its entire sense of security, as well as its very understanding of reality.

What is true is the present moment, which is timeless. Our conception of time is also an illusion, at least in the sense that we traditionally understand it. Time is not linear but rather circular and multilayered, with all moments occurring simultaneously. It exceeds the ability of the rational mind to understand, but this truth may be touched upon in moments when consciousness exceeds the ordinary waking state—for instance, in meditation or during any activity when your sense of time becomes diluted and melts away, until one moment seems to blur into another. These moments are like tiny portals to an undercurrent that allow us to catch a glimpse, however small or brief, of the sense of timelessness that underlies each moment of our daily waking lives. In these moments we are able to witness and touch upon the truth of timelessness and thus transcend the state of ordinary waking consciousness, which is entirely driven by the mind's projections of past and future. These openings are the moments when we are most deeply connected to our true self and have the clearest access to the Spirit World.

The more we can create those moments of connection and opening, the more fulfilled we will be. This is because true fulfillment cannot be attained from the outer world that exists around you. Due to the transient nature of the world, any happiness that is obtained will also be transitory and is subject to change. This is not to say that it is wrong to enjoy the variety of people and experiences in your life—quite the contrary. It is possible to savor the gifts of the world while remaining unattached to a particular outcome because you derive your sense of fulfillment not from what happens on the outside but from your sense of connection with your own being on the inside. That sense of being within you is eternal and unchanging. It is the only unchanging truth in the world of illusion that surrounds you. The more you can consciously connect with that truth through touching the timelessness of the present moment, the more you will be free to enjoy your life, regardless of what happens, and the more content you will ultimately feel.

Living in this way means getting in touch with the inner observer inside of you that witnesses the drama of life as it unfolds. In this sense, you attain the understanding that you are not the emotions, the circumstances, or the experiences of your life. None of those things truly reflect who you are. You are not those things but rather the beingness that observes them.

This awareness will deepen with the initial recognition of the false reality around you—what we are calling the veil—and the true reality within you, that which can be understood as beingness, or consciousness. In other words, at a certain point during spiritual growth and evolution, many people experience a sense of detachment or removal from the physical world around them. It is not uncommon to experience feelings of dissociation from the world, feelings of "going crazy," or feelings that the outside world seems fake or like a giant play—because in fact it is! No matter what background a person comes from, a large part of any spiritual awakening process involves waking up to the collective dream in which humanity finds itself.

As we progress upon our spiritual path, however, our understanding continues to deepen until we eventually realize that even these distinctions of true and false, of illusion and truth, of the Spirit World and the physical world, are illusions as well. While these designations are helpful to classify and define our experience, they, too, are merely projections of the ego that encourage an understanding of reality based on duality. The truth is that there is no separation between the Spirit World and the physical world; they are one and the same, merely representing opposite sides of the same coin. One reflects and sustains the other, and indeed one cannot exist without its alleged opposite.

In this same vein, even with the understanding that the world around you is an illusion comes the realization that this doesn't detract from the beauty, goodness, and divinity of the external world. The essence of the Spirit World is intertwined within the physical. We can, for instance, glimpse the essence of the Spirit World being mirrored back to us within the physical: in the smoky hues of the sunset at dawn, in the soft cooing of birds during the early morning hours, or in the musical tones of a child's laughter. The same spiritual essence is contained within the deepest caverns of our own being and can be illuminated by the light of our awareness, if we are willing to look within.

Just as the Spirit World is deeply connected to the physical realm, so, too, is the physical world deeply interconnected with the spiritual realm. In fact, the physical world is nothing but a projection that is birthed into existence from the Spirit World. Everything and everyone around you arose from the same primordial Source of consciousness, and it is back to this void that everything will return. Everything that is manifested on the physical plane is ultimately an extension of that beingness. The difference between the Spirit World and the physical world that we exist within is simply that in our physical realm, consciousness has manifested itself into form. However, initially we, too, were formless, before we chose to incarnate into bodies and take a journey into the physical, and ultimately we will once again return to formlessness, when the time comes for us to shed the physical robe of the body and journey back to our original formless state.

This same sense of oneness that connects the physical and the spiritual world also resides within us. While we may be tempted to label our ego and our higher self as being separate, in reality they are one and the same. Like the physical world around you, your ego was created by an infinite Source of consciousness, what you may understand as your higher self, or your spirit. Ancient mystics and yogis understood this timeless truth: Creator and created are one. You are both the Creator and the created, and it is only the veil of separation that prevents you from seeing this truth.

Surpassing the egoic state of your mind and connecting to the vastness within you is equivalent to seeing beyond the veil. Seeing beyond the veil, therefore, refers not only to seeing the true reality beyond the physical world around you but also to seeing beyond your sense of ego into the true reality of yourself, of who you really are. Learning to love the veil and to rejoice in the gift of the world around us, even with the knowledge that it is an illusion, is synonymous with learning to love and embrace the egoic parts of our personality. Just like the veil, so, too, was the ego created for a reason, and that reason is divine in origin. We can therefore thank and bless the veil, just as we can thank and bless our ego, for its presence in our lives and for serving as our divine teachers in our collective process of awakening.

CHAPTER TWO

I AM THAT I AM

Before you were born into this body and into physical form, you *were*. You were neither a man nor a woman, nor were you any particular nationality, religion, ethnicity, or socioeconomic status. You had no physical attributes, no personality structure per se; rather, you were simply pure consciousness in its unmanifested form. You resided in a space of pure awareness and beingness. This can be understood as the realm of your spirit, rather than that of your ego.

Everything that you perceive around you in the world was birthed from the same place you were. This place can be understood in many ways and has been assigned different names throughout the ages; some people may prefer to call it the Source, or Heaven, or the Universe, or the Infinite. For our understanding here, we will refer to it as the Void. The Void, in this respect, simply refers to the absence of physical form. It is the unmanifested space and creative potential out of which all things arise and to which all things return. You yourself are a part of this Void, and you know it intimately, on the level of your spirit. You have been to this space before, and you will return there again. It is nothing to fear, but rather something to embrace, for it is the deepest place of truth you will ever find. Indeed, it is truer than any fleeting, fluctuating, and tangible manifestations that you will find here in the physical realm.

The Void is the vacuum out of which all creation arises. If we think of the world as God's creation, a precious gift created out of divine love and joy, then all the physical manifestation we see is the paint, and the Void is the canvas onto which it is painted. The Void is the space in which you were first created, before you were the "you" that you know today. It is the realm of the Spirit World, the space beyond the veil. It is also the realm that you journey into when you fall asleep and dream at night. You are no stranger to this place, although your conscious mind may try to convince you that you are.

When we travel into the Void, we travel beyond the so-called ordinary plane of three-dimensional reality, and therefore we transcend the domain of language. Language is the tool that human beings have created in order to communicate and to help us understand reality. Without language, how could we have any conception of what was happening around us? It is our egos that yearn to construct definitions of the world to help make it easier for us to understand.

Yet there are some things that language cannot define. The Void is one of these things; it simply cannot be described in words. Journeying into the Void, as we do when we dream—when we connect with spirit, or when we leave the physical body through death—is an experience that surpasses words completely. It must be experienced in order to be understood, and it simply cannot be comprehended through the rational, thinking mind.

Words are our attempt to describe and capture the indescribable. Although words are incredibly powerful, they are also inherently limited, for how can one describe infinity? Words cannot capture the vastness of the infinite. It is so much broader, deeper, and wider than we could ever hope to describe through our limited languages. This truth can be felt, however, in moments when we surrender the need to understand logically and instead open up to our hearts and our spirit.

In the English language, the word "God" is our best attempt to describe infinity. It is the closest we can come to describing the Void, the place in which no language exists, but also the place from which all language was born. It is a paradox, a catch-22 that we cannot fully articulate, but one which we can only transcend when we let go of the mind's need to understand.

Despite this discrepancy, language is the best tool that humans have devised in order to comprehend the infinity that is the Void and to bring forth our desires and intentions from this formlessness, much in the same way that our Creator created us. As it is stated in the Bible, "In the beginning there was the Word, and the Word was with God, and the Word was God" (John 1:1, RSV). The Word is that which brings formlessness into form. It brings the intangible forth into the tangible. That is why our words are our most powerful tool for manifestation. They allow us not only to describe physical reality but also to summon our dreams and passions into our lives from the Void.

It is through language that we create the narrative of our lives. From the moment we are born onto Earth, we use words to artfully weave together a plot, or a story that becomes our own. It is the role we are playing in this lifetime, so to speak. It is as if your consciousness, having elected to journey into the physical realm and incarnate into a human body for many wonderful reasons, was handed a script once you arrived: "Hello, and welcome to Earth. Your name in this divine play is so-and-so. You will be playing the role of a Caucasian female, born to middle-class parents in a small town in Ohio. Joining you in this play are your siblings, one older brother and one younger sister. You will be playing the multiple roles of daughter, sister, friend, girlfriend…" And so on and so on.

And it is in this way that we learn to become the "I."

To conceptualize your life as a type of divine play might seem crude or strange at first. Yet if you pause to consider all of the roles you have played in your life—that of a spouse, a friend, a parent, a professional—you will realize that all these roles are temporary labels that you have been socialized into since birth. Since childhood, you were taught what it meant to be all of these things, including what was expected of you and what behaviors were encouraged and prohibited. You were then taught, oftentimes through example, to judge yourself in regards to your performance in each of the roles you played. If you judged yourself to have fulfilled your roles satisfactorily, you likely felt good; conversely, if you judged yourself to have fulfilled your roles inadequately, you likely felt as though you were lacking in some fundamental way.

These roles are merely creations of the ego, which are then mirrored back at us and reinforced by society. This is not necessarily a negative thing per se, yet it can cause suffering if we identify primarily with these egoic roles without recognizing them for what they are. In other words, if you were to go through your life believing that all of your worth was based in how "well" you performed in the role of mother or in the role of your professional career, then you would be placing your entire identity structure and worthiness in an arbitrary role that is ultimately transient.

For, ultimately, such roles are but a tiny portion of who you really are. They represent only a small fraction of the vastness of your creativity and consciousness. None of the roles that we devise for ourselves are permanent, and throughout our lives, we will shift out of some and grow into others. It is like a snake shedding its skin repeatedly as it continues to develop, evolve, and become.

You are that snake, and the shedding of the skin is akin to shedding your identification with various societal roles. During your childhood you played the role of student and child. When you grew a little older, you shed those roles and took on new ones, such as that of adolescent, college student, or possibly boyfriend or girlfriend. As you continue to grow, you will shed those roles yet again and develop new ones, such as that of a professional, a husband, wife, or parent. Again and again throughout the life cycle, you will shed your skin, so to speak, while simultaneously adopting a new skin as you evolve into different roles to play.

There can be great joy in this process—the joy of growing, chang-ing, shifting, and flowing with excitement and ease. But such joy is born out of the recognition of the roles for what they are. It is one thing to play the roles in your life while retaining awareness that you are the Creator of the play. It is quite another to become absorbed and identified with the roles entirely. It is the difference, ultimately, between staying asleep and waking up. Have you fallen asleep within the dream of your own life, forgetting that you are the dreamer?

One of the first steps to waking up out of the dream of the ego's role identification is simply learning to cultivate awareness. As we set the intention to dig a little deeper, to excavate the realms and cavities underneath the surface layer of our consciousness, we start to find a truth embedded within us that is deeper than all of the superficial roles we have been conditioned to play throughout our lives. We can begin to connect with that eternal aspect of our being, that primordial conscious awareness that was the precursor to this body and this mind—that same primordial consciousness that made the decision to embark on a journey into life in physical form. We can find this consciousness again using different meth-ods, including meditation, hypnosis, and breath work, to name but a few. Ultimately, it matters less how we find it than if we find it at all. The process of self-awakening may take some time, and everyone will get there in a different way. That deep awareness is within each of us, however, and no matter what we have been through in our lives, it is never lost.

Once we relocate that truth inside of us, that awareness of our own being, we can see with stark clarity that all the various roles we have played throughout our lives were just that: roles, like actors in a play. The impermanence of those roles then reveals itself in comparison to the abiding sense of connection, contentment, and deep peace that is accessible through touching the depths of our own being.

This is not to imply that the roles in our lives are meaningless or are something to transcend. On the contrary, once we have been granted even a glimpse of the magnificence of our own being, then we can see the roles clearly for what they are, and they become all the more meaningful and valuable to us. The roles that our souls have taken on serve to reflect back to us our inner truth—that we are the Creators of the roles and that we formulated them, out of divine love and joy, to allow us to better expand our consciousness and learn soul lessons that we scripted for ourselves to learn in this lifetime. Even though the roles are temporary and are not the ultimate truth, that doesn't negate their beauty and their purpose. In the same manner, an artist's awareness of the transience of his artwork does not detract from his creative endeavors but rather serves to mirror his own creativity and potential back to him.

Like the artist and his artwork, the Creator and the created are one. They are not separate from one another but rather are infinitely connected, with one feeding into and strengthening the other. The creative consciousness of the universe is one with who you are, just as you are one with the creative consciousness of the universe. You cannot ever separate or disconnect from this truth, for you are divine energy encapsulated in a physical body. You might understand your divine energy, or your beingness—that part of you which arose forth from the Void—to be your higher self, whereas the part of you that is your personality structure and your ego, which has been conditioned into roles to play, is your lower self. The ultimate realization, however, lies not just in identifying these two parts of your consciousness but rather in transcending the apparent separation between these two aspects of your being, for truly they are one.

This realization is referenced in the Bible with the powerful phrase, "I am that I am" (Exodus, 3:14, KJV). It is the same spiritual recognition that people of all religious traditions and backgrounds have realized throughout the ages, referring to this spiritual remembrance in many ways: waking up, nirvana, enlightenment, liberation. Ultimately, it is the unification of the higher self with the egoic self, dissolving into a sense of oneness and transcending duality. Attaining such realization need not be a difficult task or one that is relegated only to those of high spiritual status, such as Jesus; however, it does most often require carving a path that entails a daily, committed spiritual practice.

Like all spiritual endeavors, learning to sense this truth within you is an ongoing process. It is not something that can be learned overnight, nor is it something that a master teacher can teach you in one seminar or class, although others can most certainly provide you with tools for you to do the work on your own. One of the most powerful tools for connecting with that eternal space within you that transcends all egoic roles is the development of what we may call "witness consciousness."

Yogis, saints, and sages throughout the ages have cultivated the ability to enter into a witness state, whereby they watch themselves from the lens of their higher self, observing their egoic self. In this state, a person is able to simply become the observer of their own experience, witnessing their emotions, thoughts, reactions, and judgments without becoming entangled and identified with them. Once again, it is like watching the divine play of your life unfold before you while retaining your awareness that you are the Creator of the play. Rather than acting out in accordance to the drama before you, you can develop the ability to simply observe events with an attitude of calm neutrality.

This is because ultimately, when you hold the realization that you are so much more than this body and this mind, your attachment to the outcomes of events around you dissipates. For example, let's say you didn't get a call for the second interview for the job you wanted. If you feel that your entire beingness is tied to your role and your performance in your career, then you could indeed interpret this event to be devastating. If, however, you are anchored in the awareness of your being and hold an awareness of yourself as infinitely connected with the whole of creation, then such an event may become almost inconsequential, a tiny ripple in the ocean of the entirety of your experience.

It is true, however, that maintaining such an expanded awareness of yourself can be difficult, especially in the daily business of life and responsibilities. That is why it is highly valuable to develop a regular practice—whether it be meditation, guided relaxation, or journaling—that serves to connect you to that sense of expanded self so you can apply that understanding to other areas in your life. Traditionally, this has been the purpose of meditation, for in meditation a person can practice cultivating witness consciousness by detaching from the thoughts in the mind. Learning to detach from your feelings and thoughts, rather than to identify with them, is a significant step in developing witness consciousness. It is a vital step to recognize that your identity is not the emotion—no matter how intense it feels—but is rather the spaciousness and the consciousness from which that emotion arose forth, much like the original Void of creation spoken of previously. You are not the form itself but rather the spaciousness from which the form arises.

Developing the skill of witness consciousness is like developing any other skill or like working a muscle in the body. Just like with the development of a new hobby, improving this skill takes consistent practice, and you may find yourself slipping up at first. It is a practice to be undertaken with great compassion and kindness for yourself, especially as you first begin.

No matter how advanced at a skill you become, however, it is undoubtedly an ongoing practice that you may continue to improve on throughout your life. Thus, there is no final end or arrival point when you finally master the skill of witnessing your thoughts instead of becoming them. As you progress, life will continue to present you with new, challenging situations that provoke reactionary patterns that are embedded within your subconscious mind—and truly, what a gift this is! It is an ongoing opportunity to expand, to deepen your awareness and broaden your consciousness as you continue to delve into the depths of your own being. This, after all, is the journey for which we came here.

Another skill that develops from consistently practicing witness consciousness is the ability to witness yourself in the same way that Source witnesses you: with absolute clarity, unconditional love, and acceptance. As you separate yourself from your egoic thinking mind and develop the capacity to shift into the viewpoint of your higher self, so do you develop the capacity as well to view yourself in this loving manner.

For instance, let's say you are confronted with a painful situation in one of your close relationships that elicits intense emotions or thoughts for you. By choosing to shift your perspective to that of your higher self, you create a fresh vantage point from which to view the situation. You can witness the emotions without judging or labeling them; simply allow them to be there, realizing that they are an experience generated from the egoic mind and that they will pass. You may say to yourself, "I see that right now I am feeling discomfort and irritation. Let me remember that these are simply emotions, not good or bad, just feelings coursing through me, and I know they will pass." In this way, you learn to witness the sensations without completely identifying with them.

Taking this example one step further, you may, as you continue to deepen in your practice, begin to sense a distinction between your egoic self—the name and storyline associated with your body in this lifetime—and your higher self, which is eternal and all knowing. This is not to imply a fragmentation within your personality but rather to suggest an elevated level of awareness in which you become consciousness that has become aware of itself as consciousness. In other words, rather than playing the actor or actress in your own life's play, you recognize yourself as the Creator of it all.

I experienced a profound example of this after the Ayahuasca ceremony. In a moment of complete clarity, I remember gazing at myself in the mirror and saying the words, "Thank you for giving me Purandev." I felt a tremendous amount of gratitude for this beautiful soul, that which I called "myself." From a higher vantage point, I saw all of her imperfections and all the perfection within them. I saw her courage, her beauty, her heart, her insecurities— all of it—and felt only the deepest level of love for her. There was not a single ounce of judgment within any of it, only the deepest sense of tenderness and gratitude. It was the purest experience of true love I had ever felt for myself.

Reflecting on that experience, I thought often of that sentence: "Giving *me* Purandev"—what a strange thing to say! And yet it wasn't. It made perfect sense because I was so deeply connected to the realm of my higher self, which was the "me" I was referring to. I was my spirit, looking at myself in human form, with only the utmost sense of joy, love, and deep appreciation for "Purandev"— the body and being that had been given to me. Given to me by who? By the Creator, which also refers to me, because I am an extension of the Creator.

I also felt nothing but the deepest sense of gratitude for this being, "Purandev," because she had been gifted to me. "Thank you for *giving* me Purandev": this was another point I often reflected upon. "Purandev," this particular body with all of its nuances and abilities and tendencies, was *given* to me. Therefore, she does not belong to me. In fact, nothing truly belongs to us; everything in the world, including our bodies, belongs to the Creator. Everything material in our lives is ours only for a temporary time. We are doing nothing more than taking out a temporary loan on our human bodies. And when the time is right, that loan expires, and it is time to return our belongings and our bodies back to the Creator. But for some designated amount of time, whether it be twenty years or eighty years, these precious bodies are granted to us so that we can explore a life on Earth in physical form. What a precious gift that has been given to us!

These insights added a new level of richness, gratitude, and clarity to my life and profoundly impacted how I viewed not only the world around me but also myself. Suddenly I viewed myself with the same level of purity and love that the Creator felt when gazing upon me. This was very different from the way I was used to perceiving myself, and it was certainly not the way that society had ever taught me to think about my own self-worth.

No matter what we have been taught or what we think about ourselves, it is possible for all of us to open up to this level of self-love and appreciation in our daily lives, and it is not necessary for us to undergo a radical spiritual awakening to do so. We can start by simply beginning to cultivate that witness state within ourselves and practicing maintaining that state whenever a challenging moment arises. We can practice developing a sense of loving awareness of ourselves by finding the grace to shower ourselves with forgiveness rather than holding ourselves guilty and accountable for all of the various ways we deemed ourselves to have "messed up." This state of love and compassion is, after all, the same state that the Creator holds when witnessing us. Why then should we hold ourselves to a different standard? It is simply a matter of the Creator witnessing its own creation. Your higher self is the Creator of your consciousness, and your ego is the creation.

This level of self-awareness and remembrance of your true identity is what is meant by the spiritual term "liberation." It is nothing fancier than that. It simply refers to waking up to that which you truly are, which is infinite spirit, and retaining that remembrance and infusing it into your daily life. Such a shift in perspective is deeply powerful and has the ability not only to change your life but to redeem the world. It begins with one person at a time, and it starts with you.

Whisper to yourself the gentle reminder: "I am that I am." I am not the roles I play, I am not the clothes I wear, I am not my job, I am not my body, I am not my mind. *I am* the eternal, abiding consciousness behind the roles. I am the Creator of the play. Remembering this just once a day is enough to shift your consciousness. Allow the mantra to course through you like a wave with every step you take, with each pulsation of your heart, guiding you back home to your true self once again.

CHAPTER THREE

FORGETTING AND REMEMBERING

The journey of remembering and reclaiming your spiritual identity is just that—a journey. Like any worthwhile journey, it will inevitably present you with various obstacles, surprises, and detours along the way.

Throughout your life you may experience moments, or perhaps extended time periods, of increased clarity and understanding about who you are, your life purpose, and why you are here. You may abide in this understanding for a brief time until this awareness begins to drift away again, and you find yourself gradually being pulled back into the dream of unconsciousness. Much like the ocean tides or the stages of the moon, so, too, does our spiritual growth and understanding tend to wax and wane. Rather than condemning this natural and rhythmic cycle as "bad" or as a "regression" of progress on your path, it is important to realize that *all* of it is a part of the inherent cycle, the natural ebb and flow of forgetting and remembering.

We could perhaps go so far as to say that after awakening occurs, the true work begins, because while you may experience a deep shift within your consciousness and a recognition of your true identity, in many ways the world around you remains the same. While it is true that your awakening contributes to and affects the awakening of the planet as a whole, the fact remains that those around you are most likely still "asleep" within the confines of their own unconscious dream—and therefore it is necessary for you to function and relate to others from your awakened state in a world that is still largely asleep.

Maintaining your awareness and living in remembrance of your true divinity while functioning in the world becomes the practice. While this practice is straightforward, it is not easy. It is not easy because of the slippery nature of the mind and its innate pull toward duality and polarization, which only becomes stronger and more pronounced when that tendency toward forgetfulness is mirrored back constantly by the world around you.

The mind will inevitably attempt to pull you back into the dream. It is necessary to gain awareness of this so you can recognize and learn to prevent it when it is happening. Rather than judging or criticizing yourself when this natural tendency arises, simply notice it with a great deal of compassion for yourself. The work of remembrance is oftentimes tedious and requires great awareness, focus, and discipline. For this reason it could be said that the true work of spiritual practice is about remembering. Regardless of what religious or spiritual background you connect with, all the various practices ultimately aim to bring you back to the same place: that place of lifting the veil of amnesia, of retaining your original remembrance of exactly who you truly are, of recognizing yourself as consciousness waking up to itself as consciousness.

It can become especially difficult to stay engaged in this remembrance process amid the torrent of daily responsibilities, only some of which may include a full-time job and caring for children and other loved ones. In today's world, we can become so overwhelmed with the demands on our time and attention that we seldom even allow ourselves a moment of pause to breathe and gift ourselves the blessings of self-care. As a result of the reality we find ourselves in, it becomes important to manage our expectations as we progress along our path. Is it reasonable to assume that we can maintain an enlightened state within every encounter and experience that we find ourselves in? Is it reasonable to believe that we should be able to remember and act, at all times, from that place of inner truth and wisdom within us? Or is it more reasonable and perhaps kinder to admit to ourselves that we are not "perfect," that we will experience periods of forgetfulness? In my own journey of forgetting and remembering, I have come to realize that what's important is not so much that we remember our truth at all times, but rather that we recognize when we are able to come back to that truth at all.

It is not necessary for us to become enlightened monks or spiritual masters overnight, or to achieve enlightenment within our lifetime. In fact, better yet that we not set out to achieve anything at all. What we call awakening is not so much something to obtain or do but rather a way of being and living in accordance with the awareness of our truth—that we are vastly more infinite than either the physical body or the temporary fluctuations of the mind that we ordinarily tend to dwell within.

Along these same lines, we need not compare ourselves unfavorably to the great masters throughout the ages, although we can certainly learn from them. Ultimately, it does us no good to compare ourselves to others, for comparison only leads to suffering. We must remember that the spiritual masters or other people in our life to whom we compare ourselves—to whom we may even feel lacking in comparison—also experienced their own trials and tribulations, and that they, too, experienced a journey of remembering and forgetting their truth.

This process of remembering and forgetting our spiritual identity serves a purpose. Understanding the purpose of this cycle allows us to open up to the gifts it has to offer, rather than lapsing into judgment when we feel ourselves falling prey to forgetting once again. Indeed, there would be no point in the journey if you didn't forget in the first place. It would be like setting out to hike a beautiful mountain and just going straight to the top, therefore missing out on all the lovely sights, sounds, and sensations along the way. If you skipped the entire trek up the mountain, you would miss the entire point—which is the journey itself.

Much like the trek up the mountain, the point of your life is not about making it to the top; nor is not about achievement or outcome. The point of your life is about the journey you went through to get there. It's about the learning, growth, and expansion that occurs through the people you meet, the relationships you develop, and the successes and failures you draw to yourself through the experiences you create. It's about allowing yourself to experience the vast array of human emotions as you engage wholeheartedly, through the entirety of your being, with the process of life. It's about absolving karma and learning the lessons that your soul charted to learn before you incarnated into human form.

If you somehow made it to the top of the mountain first, how would you ever learn any of these beautiful lessons? The only way to learn them is through your experience—through putting one foot in front of the other, step by step, climbing up the mountain toward the peak, soaking up the myriad of sights and sensations around you along the way. This is the way that my sister Ally hiked the mountains of New Zealand, taking in each precious sight and all the sensations that the hike had to offer. She understood: going straight to the top of the mountain would be missing the entire point!

Before your soul incarnated into this human body, you knew the veil of illusion would descend upon you. This knowledge is part of the agreement that we make as we incarnate into our human existence. We come into this world with perfect clarity, understanding entirely the unfolding of our consciousness, knowing also with perfect clarity that we will soon forget everything our souls knew in the Spirit World. We agree to forget it all, in fact, because we know that forgetting is the only way for us to learn what we need to learn. Forgetting is an integral and necessary part of the process.

Life on Earth is the school that our souls attend to learn lessons and expand our consciousness. What would be the point in going to school and learning if, once you got there, your teacher provided you with all the answers before the test? How would you ever be able to measure what you had learned? Much like children in school are tested, so, too, are our souls tested in this "Earth school." We are tested in various ways, such as in our relationships, our jobs, and virtually all aspects of our lives. Forgetting in this context allows the lessons—spiritual lessons of self-love, forgiveness, trust, and empowerment—to be richer, more meaningful, and ultimately more real. The amnesia that we experience as we are born is necessary to bring these lessons about.

That is not to say that the veil cannot be pierced through and transcended; indeed, doing so allows us to regain that original remembrance of our spiritual essence and truth. Remembering our spiritual identity is just as much a crucial part of the process as forgetting it again. Once we gain an understanding of the beauty and perfection within the cycle of remembering and forgetting, we learn how to flow through it with more ease. Rather than struggling against the part of us that tends to forget—the egoic part of the mind—we can hold a vaster picture of the function of the cycle in our minds and allow ourselves permission to flow from one spectrum to the other, knowing that even when we do forget, it is likely only a matter of time before the natural ebb of the tide kicks in and we are able to remember ourselves yet again.

Of course there are also a multitude of ways to return to your truth once you realize you have forgotten it. The more awareness you develop in regards to this cycle, the easier it will be to draw yourself back to the remembrance of your true identity as a divine being. You will find, with time and consistent practice, the methods that work best for you. You may also begin to notice particular patterns or situations that trigger a sort of amnesia to occur within you. For instance, perhaps you notice that certain arguments with your spouse regarding appropriate ways to spend finances send you into a stressed and anxious state. Yet is it the true "you" who is becoming upset by this topic, or is it the "you" that is associated with the storyline, the drama of your play? With some heartfelt consideration and inquiry, you will find that it is merely the egoic part of your personality that is creating such a reaction. It is only a fraction of your consciousness in which this reaction occurs. When you remember this and tap into the truth of yourself as the eternal "I AM" presence rather than the small, egoic "I," then you are able to consequently shift into the witness state, where you can watch the emotions without identifying with them. It becomes much easier to witness your feelings, thoughts, and fears, despite their intensity, when you recognize that they are *not you*. You are not the thoughts and feelings themselves; you are the space from which they arise.

When you realize you have forgotten or slipped back into the realm of the logic mind, some of the ways you may practice return-ing to your truth are through journaling, meditation, walking in nature, or spending time in silence. You may find that spending time in particular places, such as churches or monasteries, allows you to practice remembering in your daily life. Spending time with certain groups of people who are spiritually like-minded may also help. Perhaps you create a certain ritual that you perform every day, such as praying when you wake up in the morning, or create a designated place in your home like an altar to help connect you with your deepest spiritual essence. You may create an affirmation of your choice that you recite in the morning or throughout the day to anchor you in spiritual remembrance.

Spending time with children is also a wonderful way to ground yourself in the clarity of life beyond the veil of forgetfulness. Unlike adults around them, many children have yet to be indoctrinated by societal messages of separation and fear. Their egos have not yet developed the programs that prevent them from seeing the oneness of life. Because they have spent less time on the Earth, they are closer, so to speak, to the Source, or what we may call the Void, from which they came forth. Some children may even retain memories of what they were doing or how they felt before they were born. The purity of their imaginations and the freedom of their creative expression demonstrate the inherent joy that our spirits know in the Spirit World. We, too, know that same freedom deep down but have become weighted down with societal expectations about what we should do or how we should act that stifle our creativity and growth.

Allowing ourselves permission to open up to the creative and imaginative play of children is one of the most powerful tools we have for remembering our true nature. For the nature of our spirit is infinitely creative, joyful, and pure, much like the personality of a child. Indeed, in our hearts we are all children. Within us there is a divine spark of purity, as well as a remembrance of who we are and where we came from. That remembrance is embedded within the very code of our DNA. Although from the standpoint of the mind, that remembrance may seem hazy and distant, it is nonetheless buried within the confines of our being like a hidden treasure.

Ironically, for all of the teaching and instruction that we provide to children as they grow up, it is they who have the clearest access to the treasure buried inside. In order for us to reclaim and re-remember that treasure within us that we have forgotten, we must return to the purity and innocence of our original self. We must become like children.

It was with this type of innocence and purity that I gazed upon the world after my spiritual awakening. I remember acutely how strange it was to return "back" into my body and back into the world of physical form with all of its cultural and societal mandates. Everything around me seemed at once completely surreal and, at the same time, more real than ever. It was a feeling similar to that of lucid dreaming—I was back in the dream, but I was awake to who I was.

With time, the lucidity of my understanding dimmed. As the months piled on, it became more difficult for me to maintain the same level of spiritual clarity and insight. At first this realization bothered me, for I recognized that I was "forgetting" the spiritual truths I had learned. Yet gradually, I realized that there was nothing to fear, for I could never truly forget those spiritual truths, because they were a part of me. In fact, that truth was not something outside of me that I needed to obtain—and therefore that I could lose. Rather, that truth *was* me. *I am* the truth; therefore, I cannot lose it. How can you lose that which you are?

In your journey throughout your life—on your individual trek up the mountain—there will inevitably be many twists and turns along the way. You will have periods in your life when you feel more connected to your true self and your higher purpose. You will also experience times in your life when you feel lost, confused, or alone. No matter where you are in your journey, find the courage to bless it all. It is all there to teach you something: losing your way is teaching you what it feels like to find your way again, and finding your way is teaching you to become more and more aligned with your truest expression of yourself as a continually evolving being.

The more you can learn to let go of expectations about what you think your journey should look like, the more you will free yourself to experience the fullness of your life path as it is. So often we are taught to believe that our life will unfold in a linear and predictable way. Our society, family, and friends often provide us with messages about how our life is supposed to look, feeding us expectations, agendas, and time-tables that we buy into and feel disappointed when we don't meet, as if there is something wrong with us. Examples of this may include moving out of the house, getting married, or having a baby by a certain age. If we are on a spiritual path, we may expect ourselves to have things figured out or we may become disappointed in ourselves if we do lapse back into forgetfulness or stray from our spiritual practice.

Truly, though, the greatest spiritual practice of all is not any meditation or mantra or technique, but rather the process of life itself. Life itself is your greatest teacher and that includes all of life in its wholeness, with all of the winding twists and turns that your journey brings. Like you, your life path is not meant to be linear but rather multidimensional—more like a spiral or a labyrinth than a straight line. This understanding allows you to release expectations about what your life should look like and open yourself up to receiving the richness that life delivers to you. You are then free to bless all of your experiences, even the events that seemingly take you out of alignment with the remembrance of your true self.

In the end, although the path may twist and turn and take you in different directions, you can never truly deviate from your path, because you *are* the path. You are the ending and the beginning, and no matter what happens on your journey, you are never lost.

CHAPTER FOUR

LOVE AND WHOLENESS

All of us, from the time we are born, are seekers. Exactly what we're seeking often remains elusive, but over time we learn to attach this sense of seeking to external factors, such as seeking the appropriate job, career path, home, friend, or spouse. When we finally find one of these factors that we thought we were searching for, we become temporarily fulfilled. We feel happy because we think we have found that evasive element that could finally fill the deep void that we have felt for so long, whether we experienced that emptiness at a conscious or an unconscious level. This is the function of the human ego; it likes to attach to various stimuli outside in the world for self-gratification. It likes grasping onto the idea of "something out there" being the answer to that longing that cries out inside each one of us.

In fact, for some time, certain outer circumstances may soothe that inner longing, but it will be fleeting. There will inevitably come a time, weeks or perhaps years down the road, when that nagging sensation will present itself in conscious awareness yet again. Most of us fall prey to the illusion and fail to recognize that sensation for what it truly is: a deep yearning for a return to wholeness. What we fail to understand is that the only place we can truly look to satisfy this yearning is not outside of ourselves but deep within the reservoirs of our own being. Only when we truly begin to source from *within* ourselves can we hope to quench the thirst of the deepest calls of our soul.

The reason that so many of us fail to heed this call is because we have fallen under the illusion of the veil. This idea of the veil implies that the world around us is a stage set up for our learning, growth, and development as souls who have chosen to incarnate into bodies at this time. The physical world, therefore, was created as the stage for our learning to take place. It is a beautiful stage indeed, filled with marvelous people, animals, and places to explore. Every crevice of our Earth is nothing short of a miracle. Yet if we steady our minds enough, if we engage in spiritual practices such as meditation on a consistent basis, we begin to remember that for all of the beauty on the Earth, our true and original home is in the Spirit World. This is the place where souls are created and the place to which they return. It is the Source of all creation, and it is the ultimate reality, beyond the linear delineations of time and space that we use to measure reality here on Earth.

Although our minds may not consciously remember this world, our spirits do. That remembrance is etched into our cellular memory and into every fiber of our being. It is this remembrance of wholeness and belonging that our souls cry out for here on Earth. It is the remembrance of beingness, of merging, of perfect union with the Source that we miss so much on this physical plane. There is no substitute for it on Earth. There is nothing external that can ever satiate that deep, inner yearning—no person, no event, no amount of money or circumstance can close that gap. Indeed, by attempting to fill that longing with such things, we only create more suffering and unhappiness for ourselves.

To find a sense of fulfillment in our physical bodies, we must look within and cultivate a relationship with our spirit. Unlike the physical body, the spirit is immune to wear and tear. It is immune to pain and suffering; it is eternally whole, complete, and blissful. It is the aspect of our consciousness that never dies. It is infinite beyond measure and contains all the answers we seek. Within the domain of our spirit, there is nothing lacking, because the spirit transcends the egoic mind. It is pure consciousness, pure awareness—*beingness* in its original and pure form. Our spirit is our true identity, and it is the identity to which we return when we discard the physical robe of the body after death.

Only by cultivating a relationship with this part of ourselves can we ever truly be fulfilled while living life on the physical plane. Too many of us neglect this aspect of ourselves, and in doing so, we neglect the very core of our being. We forget our very essence, that which we truly are beyond the body and mind. We are paying dearly for this forgetfulness in many ways.

One of the ways we pay for this forgetfulness is within the realm of intimate relationships. The relationships we forge with others in this lifetime hold the potential to become some of the deepest sources of joy, connection, and tenderness that this physical existence holds for us. They also hold potential for some of the most painful experiences we have within this human realm, although with such experiences also comes the greatest potential for learning.

Whether we are with a partner or not, we are liable to run into difficulties and create suffering if we are searching outside of ourselves for fulfillment. Unfortunately, this is the trap that most of us fall into at some point, because it is the message we are consistently bombarded with from our families, friends, and society. From the time we are young, and throughout our lives, we are conditioned through various social media outlets, movies, and books that it is more desirable to attract a partner than to be alone. Women are often taught about the importance of attracting a husband through their physical appearance, while men are typically conditioned to think that they must be strong and financially equipped to find the right mate. Both men and women are raised to believe that they are incomplete without a partner, that being in a relationship is superior to being alone, and that there is something wrong with them if they should find themselves single rather than in a relationship. Conversely, those who do find themselves in relationships are taught to place expectations, conditions, and ultimatums on their partner because they have been told that love is a conditional process, rather than an innate one. Because of this, many people believe that love is something that must be earned and can therefore be taken away or lost. Although it is true that these outdated stereotypes are beginning to be challenged by many people in our culture, they are still deeply embedded within the psyche of the collective consciousness.

Indeed, these very ideas contribute to the idealized "happily ever after," which is portrayed poignantly in movies and television shows. One of the reasons these stereotypes have resisted destruction, then, is because on a deep level, they fulfill the ego's desperate search for completion and wholeness. We *want* to believe in the so-called happy ending. We want to believe it is possible and plausible to find that perfect soul mate, the perfect partner or job or house that will complete us, because it seems much easier— not to mention safer and less terrifying—to swallow the idea that "something *out there* can complete me *in here*." Believing such a concept alleviates responsibility and creates dependency so that we don't have to take initiative to become the authors of our own lives and thus write the script for our own happiness and destiny.

Yet this desire for external fulfillment creates a vicious cycle in which we search, futilely, bouncing from relationship to relationship, each time setting ourselves up with expectations of our happily ever after, only to ultimately find disappointment and hurt. It matters not whether we are chasing after a romantic relationship, a particular career goal, or materialistic gain, for ultimately what we are chasing after are illusions. They are like elaborately designed hoaxes, coaxing us in subtle ways with the promise of security, stability, and happiness; yet in truth, each one is nothing more than a smoke screen that only leads us further away from that which we truly seek, which is a sense of coming home to ourselves. The concept of finding the happy ending out there is the biggest illusion of them all. In actuality, *you* are the happy ending that you seek.

To be sure, it is also entirely possible for the desire for a partner to arise from within rather than to be conditioned from without. It is natural to want to co-create life with another. Romantic relationships provide us with some of the deepest joys in life, including the opportunity to connect, to share, and to be vulnerable with one another, and when functioning in the harmonious way they are intended to, they can truly enhance our experiences in life.

Yet these joys can only truly come to us when we feel whole within ourselves first. It is therefore not the desire for a partner itself, but rather the underlying motivation for seeking a partner, which should be examined and discerned: Is your desire to find a partner a result of feeling at harmony and at peace within yourself and wanting to share and deepen that joy and love with another? Or is your desire to find a partner a result of feeling incomplete or dissatisfied within your own life and wanting to find someone to fill that void you sense within? It is an important question to ask and one that deserves to be examined truthfully, with relentless honesty. If the answer to the question is the latter, then it is likely that any relationship which comes to you will be ultimately unfulfilling, because the only person who can fill that void within is you. This goes as well for any other desires, such as a desire to attain a particular job, money, or worldly possessions.

Arriving at a place of wholeness within yourself is a crucial spiritual lesson and is part of the human experience here on Earth. It is an individual journey that everyone must take at their own pace. Personally, my search for wholeness and that sense of seeking and yearning to merge back into oneness was something I've dealt with since I was a young child. It manifested first as a fierce desire to attach to my mother—as a sort of primal desire to crawl back into her womb and experience the symbiosis within, rather than the sense of division and separation that permeated the world around me.

As I grew older, this desire for wholeness continued to present itself in the realm of romantic relationships. Throughout my twenties, I sought to find a partner who would provide me with comfort, security, and love. I was fortunate enough to find loving partners and sustained several serious relationships that fulfilled me in many ways, yet deep within me, there was always a nagging feeling that something was missing. I could never put my finger exactly on what it was, yet for all the unconditional love, support, and sacrifice on the part of my partners, it was never enough. Something was missing; something didn't quite line up. As satisfied as I was on the surface, there was an undercurrent within me that sensed there was more.

Initially, I thought the reason I wasn't fulfilled in my romantic relationships was because of my partner. I thought perhaps I hadn't found the person who was exactly "right" for me, that maybe there was someone who was an even better fit out there. While that was perhaps at least partially true, now I see that what was missing from my previous relationships was *me* and my own recognition of myself as love. I was the love that I was seeking; there was nothing outside of me, and until I realized that, I was doomed to continue repeating the cycle of unfulfilling relationships.

This realization dawned on me quite dramatically during my spiritual awakening. During this experience I transcended my ego so powerfully that I sensed myself as part of everything and everyone. I was no longer "Purandev Kaur," the twenty-six-year-old art therapist from Akron, Ohio, but rather pure, unmanifested consciousness rooted in love. I stopped seeking love and became love; in other words, the lover and the loved became one. I was no longer separate but rather both at once. There was nothing I had to get, or do, or attain, because I was everything that I was seeking. There was nowhere to go, because I had already arrived. The realization was so powerful, so all-encompassing, and so transformative that it transcended words. It was only then, after a lifetime of searching, that I finally realized the truth: I was the path that I sought. I lacked nothing and contained everything, because I *was* everything. I was whole.

This profound experience drove home for me an important point: the more we seek something from a place of lack, the less easily it comes to us because of the resistance created within our vibration. Indeed, oftentimes the sooner we stop going outside to look for "it," the more easily "it," whatever it may be, can fall into our lap through the process of grace. This paradox proved true for me, for as soon as I acknowledged the wholeness within myself and stopped seeking a partner, I effortlessly attracted one into my life.

We all have the ability to attract whatever we desire into our lives. We are mighty and powerful manifesters created by a perfect Creator. Our creations flow much more easily into our lives, however, when we reside in a place of remembering our wholeness rather than a place of worrying about our lack. This is because wholeness is our truth, whereas lack, in any form, is an illusion created by the ego.

Like any spiritual undertaking, it is a practice of awareness to discern when you are dwelling in a space of wholeness rather than lack. One of the most helpful things we can do in this regard is bring awareness to whether we are loving from our spirit, which I call "big love," or our ego, which I call "small love." This is not intended to designate one type of love as bad and the other as good; it is simply intended to help create a distinction between different experiences and levels of what we call love and what we understand love to be.

The majority of our societal definitions and conceptions of love are actually rooted in attachment and fear. Oftentimes we confuse attachment with love, and it is in this context that we refer to small love, because it is based primarily in ego. It is small love when there are conditions, expectations, and judgments associated with it: "I'll love you *if* you do this," or "If you love me, you'll do so-and-so," or "I thought you loved me, so I expected you to be like this." This type of communication may not be verbalized aloud; it may present itself more subtly in the form of subconscious thoughts that dwell just beneath the surface level of awareness, yet such thoughts still reinforce and influence certain patterns of behavior in relationships. We even place these conditions on ourselves. How often have you placed pressure on yourself or scolded yourself for not doing something you thought you were supposed to do? How many times have you felt like you were less than you should be because you didn't measure up in a particular way? All of these judgments constitute what I designate as small love. At its core this type of love is rooted in fear: fear of not being good enough, fear of not being deserving or lovable enough, fear of losing another, fear of not measuring up in some fundamental, critical way.

In this type of small love, we are liable to become absorbed in the outcome of the love or relationship because of the expectations stemming from our ego. We may therefore become more concerned with the final outcome rather than with the process of learning and growing within the relationship itself, thereby blinding ourselves to valuable learning and the true purpose and gifts that it has to offer. For example, we may become so preoccupied with whether we will stay together in a particular relationship that we completely miss the soul lessons that we were contracted to learn with that particular person.

The point is not what happens in the relationship. The point is the process of learning to love and releasing fears and obstacles to love. The process, not the outcome, is the point. Within this context, it is entirely possible for two people to complete their soul contracts with one another without getting married or spending their lives together in the way that is traditionally expected. Even though a couple may ultimately part ways, the lessons learned and the karma healed through the process is ultimately the true intention of the relationship on a soul level. This type of relationship exchange can and does happen often.

When we surrender to the process of loving rather than getting absorbed in the outcome of that love, it expands our energy and connects us more deeply to our spirit. This is because our spirit rejoices in the creativity and exhilaration of the process itself, rather than in the outcome. In fact, in this sense the outcome is inconsequential, and the process is key. Our true joy lies in the process, and it is here that we will come to intimately know and experience love without expectations.

What is love without expectations? Simply put, it's love that *just is.* It is love that defies labels and definitions. Stripping away the societal and cultural conditions of what that love should look like, all judgments of how it's supposed to appear, all associations and judgments of what that love means, allows that love to be what it is without limitations imposed upon it. All of the flashy adornments that the ego so eagerly places on love only serve to stifle it. This is because the ego wants to categorize and classify love in order to understand it. The ego wants to take what it deems to be love, place it neatly in a box with a bow on top, and declare to the world, "This is it; this is love! This is what love looks like and feels like. I've found it!" Thus anything outside the parameters of that box would automatically be rejected if it did not fit into that neat definition of love.

This, of course, is as futile a process as trying to contain the vastness and expansiveness of your spirit. It is not something that can ever be done, because, like love, your spirit is vast beyond definition. The very definition of your spirit defies understanding of the rational, thinking mind. The same is true of love, or what we may call big love. This is Love with a capital *L* that transcends all definitions that the human mind attempts to place on it. It is Love that cannot be contained, Love without conditions attached to it. It is unconditional. It cannot be earned or lost. This Love is your divine birthright; this Love is one with who you are.

Ultimately Love and your spirit are one and the same. This is the Love from which you were made and from which you came, and it is this Love to which you will one day return. Tapping into Love is more of a process of remembering than it is a process of searching.

When we reside in the vibration of big love, we reside in a place of wholeness within ourselves that translates into a sense of one-ness with all of life. That recognition of oneness eradicates any feelings of lack stemming from ego. We begin to realize our in-nate connection to all people, both known and unknown; to our ancestors who came before us and to the generations beyond us; to the animals with which we inhabit this Earth; to the elements of nature that surround and nurture us; to all places and things everywhere. This is the oneness and harmony that our spirits know so intimately from the Spirit World. It is the same sense of oneness that we seek desperately here in human bodies on Earth. We will continue to chase after illusions, playing out the game of form, until we realize that the sense of oneness—Love—that we were searching for was nestled inside of us all along. The same desire to find that oneness can be the very catalyst that awakens us to its presence within us.

Once we touch that place of wholeness within ourselves, the searching stops. There is no need for it anymore. After all, how can you need love when you realize you *are* love? How can you lose that which you are? It is impossible. This realization allows for a sense of freedom and joy within the context of a relationship. The sense of dependency dissolves, for you have realized you don't need anything from your partner because you *are* everything. This creates space that allows for a purer experience of connection between two individuals rooted in their wholeness. In this case, two individuals would then love one another from that place of freedom within them, from that same sense of freedom that arises from the realization that they need nothing from one another to be complete. From this place of wholeness, two partners can then serve as mirrors to one another to reflect back to one another the love that they are.

This process occurred in my own life after I underwent my spiritual awakening. Not only did the awakening impact my own psyche and my relationship with myself, but it also impacted my relationship with my partner. The realization of my own vastness and limitless nature hit me so hard that I recall laughing at the absurdity of it: here I was, my entire life, searching outside of myself for something to complete me, always looking for that something within others and within the context of relationships, convinced that if only I could meet the right person, then I could find it—but what was "it" I was searching for, after all? All along it was me. I was the answer I was looking for!

Ignited with this understanding, it was as if a light bulb went off within my heart. Immediately the context of my relationship with my partner shifted in a way that my ego couldn't quite identify. It felt as if my relationship had charted new, unexplored territory, like a ship beckoning new horizons on a map. Gradually, I realized that I was allowing my relationship with my partner to just be. In other words, I was resisting my ego's need to place definitions on who and what we were. Beyond the labels of "boyfriend," "girlfriend," "lover," and "relationship," there was a spaciousness that defied definition. It was in this spaciousness that I found myself, and it was here that I experienced for the first time in my life the purity of love that is allowed to breathe, to unfold beyond labels, and to simply be what it is.

This experience of love was new for me. Prior to my awakening experience, I had always adhered to my ego's desperate desire to fit my relationships into a box and place a label on them so as to grasp a better understanding of what was occurring, hence avoiding the stickiness of ambiguity that the ego tends to dislike so much. I found myself relishing the freedom of this new Love experience. Without any inclination or desire to explain that love to anyone else, or even to myself, I felt untethered in my newfound ability to simply be Love.

My partner met me in this reciprocal state, and together we mirrored back to one another the Love that we were. In other words, as I spent time and was present with my partner, my love for him was actually reflecting back to me the Love that I felt for myself and for all beings. It reflected back to me the Love that I had expanded into and become. "I'm not in love," I said to myself in wonder, "I *am* love." Such a small distinction, yet it made a world of difference.

The truth is that Love in this sense is simple. Love originating from the spirit has no agendas, no ulterior motives, no secrets or attachments or fears. It is simply an embodiment of the divine Love that emanates from the Source and the heart of creation. It is not difficult to distinguish this Love from the attachments of the ego, which more often than not becomes entangled, complicated, and weighted down by expectations and other constraints. Pure Love, in its truest sense, does not contain any of this in its vibration.

Of course, like cultivating any spiritual endeavor, cultivating a practice of loving from this place of purity is an ongoing evolution. In my own experience, I was able to maintain the vibration of Love within me and within the context of my relationship for many months. However, as relationships begin to deepen and progress, there often arise needs from both partners' egos that must be addressed in order for the relationship to move forward. This is quite natural, and it is not a process to be shunned or viewed negatively. In fact, wonderful learning can take place, and many soul lessons can be learned from the egoic issues that arise within the context of a relationship. It is the contrast created by the duality of the attachments of the ego that allows us to even know the difference and therefore recognize pure Love when we feel it. Therefore, the ebb and flow of the learning curve is one to be honored for the wisdom it brings.

The practice then quite simply becomes about returning to the wholeness within yourself. Whether it is termed wholeness or oneness or Love, the implication is the same: it is your true self, your divine birthright and identity. The Love within you is the Love that resides within all things. The more that you can bring your awareness back to this truth, the more you can live in greater harmony and alignment within yourself, within your relationships, and within the world.

Just some gentle daily reminders will suffice—perhaps an intention in the morning each day to treat yourself and others with love, or perhaps an inspiring quote or song lyric to help remind you that Love is the truth of your being. Or try relating to your partner in a new way, as if they were a precious, divine miracle manifested in physical flesh in front of you. Which of course they are! Be willing to see yourself and the relationship with new eyes and a beginner's mind. Take away the pressures and stifling conditions you place upon yourself and your partner. As soon as you allow yourself to freely be and receive love—not because of anything you *do* but simply because you *exist*—that love will trickle into all other areas of your life, including your relationships with your children, your spouse, your coworkers. They may not understand or be able to articulate the shift in you, but they will sense it, and that is enough. Your love is powerful enough to lift the vibration of the world.

You may gaze upon your reflection in the mirror, reminding yourself that the Love within you is the Love that created the very structures of the universe, that the Love within the chambers of your heart ignited the birth of mankind, that the Love within you is overflowing and pouring out of you, without restraint or fear—Love in its purest form, for you to embody and to be.

CHAPTER FIVE

MATERIALIZATION AND MANIFESTATION

Like the Source that created us, we, too, have the innate ability to create. From the time we are born as tiny infants, unable to feed or clothe ourselves, we still retain the inherent ability to create and influence the reality around us. This ability only becomes stronger as we grow. Although our creativity may range from creating various childhood experiences to creating relationships with peers and family members to creating jobs and opportunities that come our way throughout life, one common thread remains the same: that we and we alone are the generators of our experiences. There is no one else we can credit for what has been created within us and around us except ourselves.

This is because we are not separate from the Creator, but rather one with the creativity that sparked life into being. Our ancestors recognized this truth thousands of years ago: Creator and created are one. We are made in the likeness of a master Creator, a divine Source engine of consciousness that dreamed the world into being simply for the joy of it. How, then, would it make any sense to think that our own creative abilities would be any different?

Think, if you will, for a moment of an artist immersed in his craft. Imagine this artist, completely enthralled with the process of his creation, completely one with the moment. He is not thinking about the end product but rather is completely absorbed in the process itself. This is the creative process at its best, and it is this creative process from which the greatest works of art, literature, and theatre were conceived. At its purest, this is a completely ego-less process that is initiated solely for the joy of the experience. It is carried out for the love and freedom inherent in the process itself.

It is from this pure state of creativity, carried out solely for the purpose of loving and creative expansion, from which you were born.

The creative Source did not create you with any other agenda in mind. This Source did not create you intending any specific outcome. It did not create you because it was obligated or forced to do so. You were created out of the freedom that originates from the highest vibrational love imaginable.

As Creators ourselves, we, too, have the ability to manifest our own creations and watch with delight as our dreams effortlessly unfold. In fact this ability is our birthright. It is an inherent part of who we are, and it is meant to unfold from within us as naturally as we breathe in our next inhalation and breathe out our next exhalation.

All too often, however, we become blocked and stumble because we forget our birthright as divine Creators. We forget that we contain the multitude of the entire universe, for we are one with the entire universe, not separate. It is our mind that trips us up and creates problems for us, all of which stem from the illusion of separation. We may think: "I can't do this. I don't know how," "I don't have what it takes," or "I'm not one of *those* people." We may categorize groups of people into those outside of us who somehow magically have what it takes to achieve their dreams, while the rest of us simply are ill equipped to manifest our grand destiny. Or we may attribute our lack of success in certain areas of our lives to fate:

"I'm just not meant to have my own business." "I'm not supposed to find love." "I don't have what it takes to achieve my dreams."

Whatever the thought process may be, it is the thoughts themselves that hold us back from materializing the reality that we wish to create, not the orchestration of the universe. Despite what we may believe, we are not powerless victims of our circumstances, nor are we powerless puppets of a larger creative Source that controls our lives. Nothing could be further from the truth.

In fact, we are the Creators of our own lives. There is nothing outside of us; everything stems from within. The thoughts and beliefs that we create from our own minds are the building blocks of our reality. In other words, if you believe yourself to be strong and empowered, you will be. If you believe yourself capable of starting your dream business, you will be. If you believe yourself to be healthy and balanced in your body and your mind, then the universe will deliver that reality to you. And vice versa.

It goes deeper than this, however. Many of us are raised to believe that there are external rules or truths that exist in some objective worldly landscape. We are raised to think that there are particular codes of conduct or certain punishments that will fall upon us if we say or do certain things. In other words, we are taught by society that there are objective values that we are to adhere to within the world. In many cases, this was what our parents were taught to believe by their parents before them, and their parents before them, and so on.

Once we open ourselves up to recognizing ourselves as the Creators of our reality, however, we start to see that what we really consider to be the objective world is completely subjective. It is neutral, in fact. The truth is that reality is a completely neutral, blank canvas upon which we, collectively as a human species, have created certain rules and designations: "This is good; this is bad; this is what this means; this is what you're supposed to do." We have cast the paint onto the canvas in order to create structure and meaning that allows us to feel safe.

As tempting as it is for the ego to attach to the illusion of security through these beliefs, it is important to recognize that ultimately they are completely arbitrary. Indeed, one of the most fundamentals steps of spiritual awakening is waking up to the fact that the meanings, rules, and associations that have run your life are ultimately completely self-created and self-imposed.

Allowing yourself the opportunity to detach from these conditioned programs is the ultimate freedom. In creating the human species, the creative Source gave us the greatest freedom of all: the ability to choose how we want to construct our creation. Therefore, as the sovereign Creators that we are, we have the choice to decide how we wish to flow our creative energy and potential as a species: Do we wish to create and live according to arbitrary definitions and rules that cause the ego to feel safe? Or do we choose to free ourselves from the illusion that there is some omniscient presence that controls every facet of our existence? In other words, do we wish to recognize ourselves as the limitless constructers of reality that we are? The choice is ours; the choice is yours.

One person's willingness to acknowledge their own creative potential sets the stage for others to begin to recognize theirs as well. It is an awakening process that gradually gains momentum as each human being finds the courage to awaken their heart to the true power of their nature as a sovereign Creator. Once you awaken to this realization within yourself, the rest of the process becomes easy.

There is nothing that you cannot do, have, or be in your life. The only limitations that exist around you are the ones that you create for yourself. They are there because you believed in them and strengthened them through the power of your belief. Perhaps they were limitations that were passed down in your family, or limitations that you adopted during childhood. Ultimately, it does not matter where they originated from. What matters is that you had the power to create them, and only you have the power to deconstruct them. No one else can do it for you—you are the ending and the beginning. It all comes back to you.

In realizing this, it is also important to be gentle with yourself during this process of awakening. It is all too easy to scold ourselves for the things we believed in the past or for the things we did "wrong." In actuality, however, none of it is wrong. It is all a part of the path. The limitations and stumbling blocks that we created for ourselves must be honored for their divine purpose in our growth. We must realize that we created the limitations for a specific reason. For what type of a journey would it be if there were nothing to learn or overcome? How would you ever learn the karmic and soul lessons that you came here to learn?

The process of being gentle and kind to yourself during the awakening process extends to recognizing other types of subtle resistances throughout the process as well. It is no small feat to claim your identity as the Creator of your reality. In truth, acknowledging this realization can be quite terrifying, especially for people who have spent their entire lives placing their destiny and will into the hands of an unseen God whom they have been taught dictated the outcome of their lives. While such an idea may seem constrictive, it also contains an element of security within it. For if there is an omnipresent God "out there" who is the ultimate judge of what I'm able to say or do in my life, it automatically takes me off the hook, so to speak. No longer is it my responsibility to decide the way in which I wish to orchestrate my life. No longer is it my responsibility to dive into the ambiguous caverns of life outside of me and within me and find the courage to rely on my own sense of moral conduct to guide me. No longer is it my responsibility to take the initiative to create the life I want, nor do I have to gaze in the mirror and come face to face with my own creative power.

There is a saying that it is not our darkness that most frightens us but rather our light. Indeed, in many ways this is the most terrifying acknowledgment of all: that of our own identity as Creators. Sometimes there may even be a part of us that wishes to deny this truth, because deciding that circumstances are beyond our control seems far easier and absolves us of tremendous responsibility.

It is easier to remain within the confines of our constructed belief systems and corresponding comfort zones, to choose to believe that they were created for us by an all-powerful Creator, than to acknowledge that we created those self-contained boxes and beliefs ourselves. This is largely the path that humanity has chosen for the past several hundred years.

Yet now we find ourselves at the precipice of a new age of consciousness that is descending upon humanity. The time has come for us to become stronger than our fears of taking responsibility, stronger than our fears of owning our power, and stronger than our fears of stepping outside the belief systems that we have constructed for ourselves. It is time for humanity to accept our creative power—for while it may feel safer, ultimately there is nothing to gain by denying our natural ability to create the lives that we want. The power comes from taking responsibility for who we truly are. And that means also taking responsibility for what we have created and for what we are *capable* of creating.

The truth is that once we find the courage to acknowledge our divine nature despite our fears, the freedom that we experience from doing so is well worth it. This is because our true nature is freedom—the freedom to create a life that we love.

After my awakening experience, I distinctly remember feeling as though reality around me was pliable, as though I could reach into the abyss of infinity and materialize that which I wanted. I had been liberated to see beyond the veil and the illusion of maya. Because I recognized the material world around me as a smoke screen, I found the freedom to transcend it.

"My dreams flow through me; I am the key." I repeated this phase in my mind, connecting not so much to the words themselves as to the sensation of freedom within them. All fears and doubts that had been lodged within me melted away, and I experienced a sense of profound, unshakable peace. I no longer worried about controlling events or circumstances in my life because my inner and outer worlds had collided as one. In other words,

I realized there was nothing to worry about because I was creating my reality around me. I recall thinking that if there was a certain outcome I didn't want to occur within my life, I could simply choose not to allow those possibilities into my reality. It *really* was that simple. This simplicity and ease was quite a stark contrast to the way in which I was accustomed to living, as if I had to control life around me—as if I was somehow separate from life rather than one with it.

The simplicity of the manifestation process astounded me. I had never felt so empowered, so completely at ease. The realization came as effortlessly as a tiny bud unfurling into a flower. I had awakened to myself as Creator.

It is the mind that talks us out of the simplicity of existence and overcomplicates things. The mechanics of the thinking, egoic aspect of the mind tries to tell us that this process is complicated, that we are powerless, that we are somehow separate from all of creation and therefore have no say in how this divine play unfolds—as if we were watching the play rather than directing it.

All that is required of you is to open to the recognition of your divinity. It is not necessary for you to be a guru in the mountains of Tibet, or a yogi chanting Sanskrit mantras all day long, or anyone doing anything other than what you are doing right now. In fact, who you are and what you are doing right now is perfect.

In recent years there has been much talk about the law of attraction. Simply stated, the law teaches that what you think about is what you draw to yourself and manifest into your life. The thoughts you think act as magnets that attract situations, people, and events into your life that match those thoughts. This is because like attracts like.

Our ancestors knew this law many years ago, but with the rise of technology, it was largely forgotten within the collective consciousness. Before the development of technology, our ancestors knew what it meant to create their reality by utilizing the elements of nature—using sticks and rocks to build a fire, for instance.

They saw themselves not as separate from nature, but as one with it, and this realization connected them to a deep understanding of their own generative and creative power. Conversely, modern society has become increasingly dependent on the use of technology, which has decreased our connection to the elements of nature and has led us to forget our innate ability to sculpt and construct our reality around us. Although technology has made modern life easier for us in innumerable ways, it has also led us down a path in which we have deferred to giving away our power to devices and computers that we believe hold the answers for us. It is one of the factors that has contributed to us forgetting the deep reservoir of manifestation power that we hold.

Recently, however, humanity has begun to awaken from its dream of victimhood and reclaim its creative power once again. The law of attraction has surfaced back into the collective consciousness and has received a resurgence of validation for the truth and power that it holds.

While the law of attraction teaches a fundamental truth, oftentimes we are only familiar with one part of the equation. You may think positive thoughts every day, all day, but if you do not recognize yourself as divine and as the Creator of your experience, then you will only be able to go in so deep. It is like going scuba diving in the ocean but staying tethered to the first fifty feet from the shore. There is so much more depth and beauty to experience. So the aspect of the law of attraction that we are most familiar with in our society today is only the tip of the iceberg.

To go deeper into exploring your divine creativity means not only manifesting the reality that you want but *materializing* it. Materialization is the next stepping-stone after manifestation that can only be arrived at by recognizing yourself as the Source. The power of the universe opens up to you when you recognize who and what you *are*. Once you understand who and what you are, then you are free to create. You become limitless, because even though you are within a temporary human body—designed of your own creation—you are connected to that limitless aspect that dwells within you, outside the constraints of time and space. Connecting to that limitless aspect within your being opens you up to the endless flow of creativity that pours forth from the Source.

When you are attuned to this space, not only are you free to create like the Creator, but your creations will be imbued with deep love and joy. Just as the Creator created you in love, so, too, does love become the motivation for all of your creations. You create in your life for the sake of creating, simply because you have been given the ability to do so. This is the purest type of creation, because it is free from the obligatory grip of the ego. There is no "should" in the vibration of the creation, no "I have to" or "I need to" or even "it needs to be like this." Having tapped into your own creative Source energy, you simply wish to create situations, relationships, and adventures in your life because you can—for the pure love of it. Creations stemming from this vibration are infinitely more powerful than creations that are motivated out of a sense of obligation or fear. They have a greater chance of truly sticking long term, as well. Such materializations will also undoubtably be more satisfying to your spirit.

The process of materialization truly is simple. All that is required of you to materialize that which you desire is your *intention* and *attention*. Through these two key processes, materialization takes care of itself quite naturally.

To start, it is helpful to set an intention to guide the energy in the direction you wish for it to flow. Our intentions, similar to our beliefs, serve as the building blocks of reality. They assist us in harnessing the infinite Source energy that is accessible to us at all times and directing that energy to a particular place. It is like an artist who declares she wishes to paint a picture of a tree. By setting the intention to paint a tree, she has shed the excess space on the page and created a structure and frame from which to operate. That does not mean that the tree painting will end up looking exactly the way she originally intended, and that is okay. There is always room for creative licensing and improvisation.

Like the artist above, you may set the intention to find a job that allows you to pursue your love of traveling. Having set your *intention* on finding this job, you would then begin to place your *attention* on it by thinking about it, talking about it with others, and conducting a job search. You would devote a substantial portion of your attention to your intention of finding this job. Every moment that you spend thinking of it and placing your attention on it strengthens the magnetic force of your thoughts and anchors them in physical reality.

Rather than becoming stuck within expectations about what the job should look like or prescribed notions of where the job will come from, such a person would be wise to surrender these concerns to the flow of the universe, out of the reign of their individual ego, and to trust that the creative Source will co-create with the creative potential of her own higher self to deliver something that is a thousand times more aligned than she ever could have dreamed possible.

The final element of the process of materialization reiterates what was stated before: to recognize yourself as one with the divine Creator. This sounds straightforward but is often the most difficult and overlooked part, for we are not raised to look at ourselves in the mirror and see divinity. Nor are we raised to bow forward in humility at our own divine grace and creative potential. In actuality, it is quite the opposite: we are told in subtle or not-so-subtle ways from a very young age that we are inept, not good enough, not worthy enough, and incapable of achieving our dreams. Most of these false illusions and distorted beliefs were passed on to us from our parents, whose parents were taught the same from their parents, and so on. If we are truly committed to breaking the cycle of denying our divine creative power, then we must be willing to acknowledge ourselves as the Creator.

These are the three requirements within the equation of materialization: harnessing intention, placing attention, and anchoring your awareness to your own authentic divinity. These elements work together like a mathematical equation that, when properly applied, will work every time.

The underlying basis of materialization is freedom. In this context, love and freedom can be understood to be the same thing because they vibrate at the same frequency. The Creator created you out of divine love that expanded because it wished to know itself. The basis of this divine love that was given to you is freedom: the freedom to create. Just like the universal love that created you, you were endowed with the same free will that ignited all of creation.

In your creation, you were granted the free will to design your body, your life, and your karmic lessons. You were given freedom to design and select, with full conscious intent and awareness, your challenges, your struggles, your triumphs, and your dreams. Of course you were provided with guidance from your guides and soul group, but ultimately the choices you made were yours. You were the artist of your own life before you were born, and you are the artist of your life now within the context of this lifetime.

To illustrate this inherent freedom within you, let's try an exercise. Imagine a room filled with multiple doors. All around you and everywhere you look there are doors: big doors, small doors, doors of varying colors, shapes, and sizes. They are all closed, and you know you can open them if you wish. Behind each door lies a different path containing a different route for you to choose in your life. They all lead somewhere different, and none are right and none are wrong. You are in what we will call the Room of Potential Realities.

Through your intention and attention, you select a path and a door. When you choose to place your attention on one door, it begins to open for you. Your intention and attention create magnetic frequencies and thought waves that draw that particular potential reality to you. You, of course, are the Creator of all the potential realities behind the doors. You set these possibilities up for yourself before you incarnated and took the journey into physical form.

The key point here is that you get to choose in freedom. You have been granted the freedom to choose, as the powerful Creator that you are, the paths that you materialize into your life. There is no reason to be fearful or overwhelmed, for the internal compass of joy is your guide. You know which doors to focus on and which to leave alone simply by observing the amount of joy that you feel at each door.

There is no way you can make a mistake. The doors may lead to different situations, different people, and different outcomes, yet ultimately they are but different rivers flowing back into the same great waters. The path is not outside of you; it *is* you. You are literally creating the path as you go.

This Room of Potential Realities exists in your life. It is operating at a subtle level beneath your conscious awareness every day. It is the operating force of reality, the blueprint of materialization, the mathematical equation of the universe. Rather than something to be afraid of or baffled by, it is something to be cherished for the majesty of its design.

The job upon which you set your intention and attention will come to you through one of these doors. For instance, if you find a job opening that fits your search criteria in a different city and begin making plans to take that job, that particular door begins to open and the other doors begin to close. This is not to say that the other doors go away; rather, they simply begin to contract, and the door that you are focusing your attention on begins to expand. It is a necessary part of the materialization process. Eventually, should you decide to walk through the door that you focused your attention on, you will step through and draw an entirely new set of unopened doors to you that are conceived from the experience. And so it continues.

The more awareness you bring to your creations and to yourself as the Creator of them, the more fluidly they will flow into your life. You will then find a way to dance in the Room of Potential Realities and to abide in the joyful flow of creation itself. Instead of struggling against the current of life, you will learn to recognize yourself as one with that flow and surrender to it.

There is nothing more powerful than awakening to yourself as the infinite Source energy that catalyzes all of creation. Awakening to yourself in this manner is the key to your freedom. It is from this space of freedom that you may embrace all the possibilities that are available to you—and like the divine artist that you are, you get to create them in the spirit of deep love, motivated by nothing more than the inherent joy of the creative Source expressing itself in form.

CHAPTER SIX

QUALITIES OF SOURCE

All of the world religions since the dawn of time have attempted to capture the essence of the Source. Throughout the ages this Source has been described by innumerable names in various languages. In our society today, we may know it as God, Allah, Jesus, Nirvana, the Source, Adonai, and so forth. There are as many names to describe the one formless Source of all life as there are differences in our ability to perceive it. In any case, the one we seek to name is beyond all of the names we assign. It is nameless, just as it is formless. What we are talking about is the ineffable mystery of creation whose infinite power and nature truly lies beyond the comprehension of the mind. Therefore, in actuality it is for ourselves that we assign labels and names to that which cannot be named. It is to satiate the desire of our ego, to satisfy its wish to catch hold of something tangible, rather than to face the alternative: to be present and open up to the inherent groundlessness of the mystery of the Source of life.

Countless wars, battles, and lives have been sacrificed in the defense of the particular religions and names of the Source. This is because humanity suffers from a disease of the mind in which it feels the need to defend "God" as it is defined in their particular tradition. Yet is it reasonable to think that the Source that birthed all of creation from its sovereign free will, which is responsible for generating and destroying universes across the cosmos, needs any defense? Is it logical to feel justified in humanity's determination to "prove" that one religion or definition of this Source is somehow truer than the rest? The question is rhetorical and answers itself, just as the ever-flowing and ever-present Source of Creation constantly answers for itself through its glorious and continuous creation of more life.

Who is it, then, that humanity is truly trying to defend in our endless battles and wars? It is not the God of our understanding that we seek to protect; rather it is our own egos, defenses, and fears that are the origin of humanity's ailments. It is our own prejudice against the other, for the underlying fear that they are somehow more worthy and more divine than us. It is our own insecurity that fuels the need to convince ourselves that our group is right in our definition of what God is and that the other group is wrong. It is our own pain and terror at the notion of setting aside our belief systems—which we so desperately cling to in an effort to feel grounded and secure in our world.

In other words, it is not the many different explanations and understandings of what Source is that is the problem. It is rather our ferocious clinging to our own definition as the right one and our labeling all the others as the wrong ones. The problem lies in our inability to let go of our fear-based conditioning, which prevents us from perceiving the many different names of God for what they truly are: different qualities of Source, each one valid and true in its own right, each one not detracting from but rather enhancing the one before it.

All of the countless paradigms and various ways for understanding the unknowable are like different facets of a glistening gem; each one sparkles with its own kernel of truth. The truth we are attempting to define is so multifaceted and complex that for us to assume that it could be captured by one singular religion or outlook is preposterous. This is not to deny the validity of any or all religious paths. It is simply to recognize that we cannot begin to perceive the complexity of the Source while looking at it through the lens of duality.

To begin to shift into a new paradigm and higher understanding of Source, we must recognize that all of the paths are true and none of them are true. These qualities of truth and untruth exist simultaneously. What rings as true to one person doesn't ring as true to another, and one person's recognition of truth in a particular religion or outlook does not negate another person's experience of truth in a different outlook. The two truths can coexist simultaneously.

The reason that it remains difficult for our minds to function under this understanding of apparent paradox is because humanity is largely operating under the lens of dualistic thinking. This type of thinking originates from the ego and assumes that if one paradigm is judged to be true, then the other is automatically understood to be untrue. Such dualistic thinking is largely how humans for centuries have understood the world: in terms of darkness and light, right and wrong, good and bad, death and life, women and men, and so forth. It is not that dualistic thinking is bad per se; however, it is massively limiting and must be broken through in order to attain a deeper understanding of the Source, which exists beyond all paradigms of duality. In fact the Source is all of the dualities and is none of them at the same time.

During the period of my spiritual awakening, the qualities of Source became very clear to me. I saw and understood the world through Source, or the perspective of my own spirit, as my ego was completely removed from the equation. Therefore, there was no "I" to judge things as good or bad or right or wrong. Everything within me and around me just *was*, and all of it existed simultaneously. The apparent paradoxes of reality no longer applied, for I was no longer dwelling within the dualistic mind. It is judgment that facilitates dualistic thinking and categorization. Within my awakened state, I was beyond judgment and thus beyond duality.

All of the apparent dualities, which I recognized ultimately as an illusion, simply faded away, giving me a direct experience of what felt to me like the truest experience I had ever encountered.

For example, rather than viewing the Spirit World as separate from the physical world in which I found myself, I suddenly understood them to be one and the same. The dualistic thinking of "here" and "there" shifted, and I understood that everything existed simultaneously and was one. A sense of timelessness permeated my days, and rather than abiding by minutes and hours, I was instead guided by a continuous flow of timeless moments. I understood past, present, and future to be held within the space of the timeless present.

Another example that unfolded after my awakening was that I no longer divided my ego and my spirit in a dualistic fashion. Instead, my higher self merged with my egoic consciousness, and I understood them to be united. The Creator in me created the consciousness that I labeled and called "Emily" in the world, but truly both versions were extensions of the Source.

What these experiences provided for me was a reconciliation of the dualistic mind and the apparent paradox that accompanies it. The deeper we explore the heart of reality, the more we come into contact with this apparent paradox. Indeed, it could be said that perhaps paradox is reality. However, the paradox only exists when we are viewing it through the egoic mind, which sees everything through the perspective of duality. When we step out of this perspective, what appeared to be paradox before now makes complete sense.

Dualistic thinking is not something to be shunned or labeled as "bad," however. Duality in itself has the potential to breed division, hatred, and fear in the world because it separates people by labeling some people as "them" out there and "us" in here. This viewpoint has been the origin of conflicts for eons and is undeniably detrimental to the evolution of humanity as a species. Yet if you strip all of the judgment away from duality, what you are left with is simply contrast, or polarities. Contrast is the appearance of apparent opposites that are barren of judgment. This type of contrast is the very fabric of our universe.

The universe in which we live expresses itself through contrast: night and day, warmth and cold, darkness and light, life and death. These polarities allow us to understand and define one another. There is a popular expression that you would never appreciate the rainbow without weathering the storm. The same is true for all polarities. How could you understand what day is without knowing its opposite—night? How could you know what light feels like without experiencing darkness? How could you know what a woman is without knowing her counterpart of man? Similarly, without knowing the confines of your human body manifested as your ego, you could never know the vastness of your spirit.

For this reason, creation—or what we may call the Source—manifested itself into polarities, at least in the realm in which we operate. These polarities exist in order for the other to see and recognize itself. Consider if you only had the quality of one of the polarities without anything to compare it to; if, for instance, you only ever lived in the daytime without ever seeing the night. Without that contrast provided for you, you would never develop an understanding of what night was because you had never experienced it in relation to light. It is through contrast that we develop, that we gain wisdom and understanding, and that we can ultimately recognize ourselves. The contrast provides the mirror from which we can look through at the "other" and see our own reflection gazing back at us.

It was this desire for self-realization and recognition that propelled creation into being. The Creator wished to know itself. The only way for the One Creator to know itself was to become many. For this reason, the One became the many.

It was necessary for the One to become many because no division exists within the Source. Neither does any judgment, duality, or fragmentation of any kind. Within the Spirit World, there is simply pure love. It is the essence of the Creator and the very heart of the universe. The foundational blocks of reality are imbued with divine love. Within this divine love there is only oneness. This quality of oneness may also be understood as love, for oneness and love are synonymous. Within the framework of love, there is no recognition of the other, or of someone being separate or apart from you. All is connected and is merged into one unified flow of ever-present, ever-flowing love. It is only when we incarnate into bodies from this space of oneness that we develop a sense of an individual "I," or what we know as the ego.

Without the development of that individual "I," how could you ever recognize yourself? You could not, because there would be no "I" to recognize. It would be impossible. Therefore, in order for Source to recognize itself, to hold up a mirror on its own divinity, it was necessary to create multiple forms from the one formless Source.

One may wonder why the Source wished to recognize and know itself. Surely a Creator as omnipresent as this would already know itself? Surely there is truly no real need for the infinite Source of Creation to manifest life forms out of its free will to reveal itself back to itself? Surely, such an all-powerful Creator would be content to just exist in oneness and love for all eternity.

The answer is as simple as it is profound. In much the same way an artist chooses to create a painting, the Source chose to create its creation out of divinely inspired love. In other words, the Source of Creation overflowed with joy, and it required an expression for that joy.

You are that expression.

Recall a time in your life when you experienced deep love and joy. Perhaps this was your wedding day, the birth of your child, an accomplishment you had worked for, a time when you were traveling or were outside in nature and feeling aligned with your higher purpose. Think of how you felt in that moment: perhaps as though you wished to hug someone, to cry, to celebrate, to announce your joy to the world—in other words, to express that love in some fashion. When the vessel of your body is overflowing with joy, it is natural to wish to express that joy and to make it manifest in the world.

This is precisely what the Source did when it created its creation. We came forth as an expression of that overflowing love, as an embodiment of it, into our human forms. Like an artist painting and reveling in the joy of his creation, so, too, does the Source revel in our presence and rejoice in our human existence.

As Source created humanity, creation was expanded. The creation of more life expands the universe rather than detracts from it in any way. There was no price that came with your human incarnation, no bargain made, and no external motivation for creating your human body other than that of providing an expression of the infinite divine love and truth of the totality, pouring into and igniting your flesh and bones.

There is a Sanskrit mantra that captures this sentiment: *Om Purnamadah, Purnamidam, Purnat Purnamudachyate. Purnasya Purnamadaya Purnameva vashisyate. Om, shanti, shanti, shanti.* In this context, *purna* translates to wholeness, fullness, or completeness. What this mantra, which serves as an ancient truth emanating from the heart of Source, teaches is this: "That is complete, this is complete, from the completeness comes the completeness. If completeness is taken away from completeness, only completeness remains."

The Source, or what we may call God, is an infinite well of creativity and potential which will never run dry. Creating new life does not detract from life. In fact it only enhances it, just as the light of one candle doesn't detract from but rather brightens another. Fullness only creates more fullness, just as love only creates more love.

Love expands the very fabric of the universe. When you choose to love yourself or to love another, the world is expanded by that love, and all of creation benefits. It creates more expansion and fullness because it is the very stuff the entire universe was founded upon. Similarly, it is the very material you are made up of. This is why we so deeply resonate with the vibration of love: it is our very essence, etched into our cellular DNA by the all-loving Creator that created us. In other words, as humans we recognize and seek pure love on a deep level because it is who we truly are. Conversely, anything that is not love—such as vengeance, jealousy, fear, or hate—causes a tear in the fabric of our being. It feels uncomfortable to us because it is misaligned with our true nature. Learning to release the things which we are not and to harmonize with the vibration of love that contains our very essence is like aligning a tuning fork to its true pitch: it feels like returning home.

Even those people who have erected walls and defenses against allowing love in as a result of insecurity cannot resist the call of their hearts to recognize love as their true nature. This is because there is nothing in the universe that is an exception to the all-powerful Love that birthed creation into being. It simply is not possible. To be sure, there are people and institutions that have disconnected themselves so profoundly from the stream of ever-present love that it would seem otherwise. However, nothing and no one in creation can truly be devoid of the divine love that births worlds into being.

Humanity's notion of a wrathful and punitive God figure, then, is out of alignment with the truth of Source. Like the many different names and paradigms of God that humanity has erected in order to understand the incomprehensible, it, too, is an illusion and ultimately reveals more about humanity's own projected fears and conflicted belief systems than it reveals any truth about the Source. The tales about an angry God in the Old and New Testament, which many of us today are familiar with, were nothing more than a way for humanity to project its desire for control onto an authoritative Godhead who punished humanity for their sins. To be sure, it undoubtedly feels safer to the ego to rest in a belief system that relies on the dualistic thinking of "good and bad" and "right and wrong." It is uncomfortable and certainly untraditional, particularly in the society we live in today, to admit that perhaps things are not as clear-cut as this and that humanity's desire to project anger onto an authoritative supreme being stems from the ego's need to have defined answers.

Indeed, it is far scarier to realize that the belief systems that have been handed down for generations are no more than a smoke screen that serves to cover up the scary truth: that the dualistic method of dividing heaven and hell is no more than a feeble attempt to categorize qualities of the Source in a way that the human mind can understand. In the same way a child learns to label different behaviors as right or wrong, so, too, has humanity created a structure for itself to attempt to understand the qualities of Source.

The problem with this belief structure is that it heralds one plane—heaven—as a part of the Source, which automatically assumes that its opposite—hell—is severed from the Source. The wrathful God punishes "sinners," those who are deemed somehow separate or cut off from the infinite Source of Love from which they came as a result of their actions; on the other hand, this same God favors and rewards those who abide by his word. This type of thinking automatically denotes some people and types of behavior as part of Source and the others as not, because it uses a dualistic approach. This paradigm has caused humanity much unnecessary grief and continues to do so today.

How could God, the Source, possibly separate anything from its wholeness? How could that which created the cosmos become severed from that which it created? How could Source become severed from Source? It is simply not possible. It is not possible because everything and everyone originates from Source. There is nothing in the world that is separate from it.

In Sikhism there is a mantra that captures this truth: *Ek Ong Kar*, which translates to "it is all one." From the one came the many, and from the many came the one. Nothing within the world can become separated from that which birthed it into being.

Therefore, it is simply impossible for people of different faiths, religions, or ethnic backgrounds to claim that one group is divinely anointed and one is not. *Ek Ong Kar:* it is all one.

To be sure, there are some people and beings who choose to live their lives out of alignment with the goodness that exists inside them. We may see these people, who are electing to engage in actions such as thievery, brutality, and violence and wonder how they can still be aligned with Source while committing such volatile acts. What becomes crucial to understand in such situations is that all of creation originates from Source; therefore, that refers to the darkness as well as the light. Darkness is simply the opposite of light. They are polarities that reflect and define one another. When we become attached to the light, however, it becomes easy to overlook and to forget that the darkness, too, is a part of Source. It exists within the fabric of creation, does it not? Therefore, it was also seeded from the infinite totality of the Source.

It is only when we judge the polarities of light and dark that we begin to creep into the terrain of duality. For instance, when we become attached to the light in the world and label it as "good" and thus create resistance surrounding the dark and label it as "bad," we create suffering and division for ourselves. Inherently, the light and dark are not good or bad; they just *are*. When we can see them as such and create enough space in our minds to simply allow both the light and the dark to be what they are, we develop the capacity to see their place within the whole. In this sense, it becomes easier to understand that even people who have committed what we might judge to be sinful actions are not separate from Source. They have simply become so blocked and disconnected from their true nature as loving and divine beings that they can justify acting in ways that are out of alignment with their truth. Viewing these actions from this perspective may elicit greater understanding and even compassion for such people.

As humanity's collective consciousness begins to evolve, so does our understanding and definition of the Source. In the past there was a time when humanity chose to become engrossed within the play of duality and erected confining and suppressing belief structures for itself; however, that time is no more. Humanity has completed and outgrown that lesson within its evolutionary progression as a species, and now a new chapter is unfolding. This chapter touts the polarities of Source not as a method of division and separation, but rather as a method of allowing recognition of the wholeness of the other. Humanity is being called to embrace the inherent divinity of all things and all beings, no matter how different one might appear to be on the surface. In recognizing the divinity of the other, we automatically claim and recognize the same divinity within ourselves.

The Spirit World rejoices in our conscious recognition of our divinity. In Sanskrit there is a word for this realization: smriti. This term refers to the joy that we feel as we remember our true nature as divine beings. We are meant to attain this realization; indeed, it is set up for us to do so. That is why the Source established a system of polarities and of opposites in the world, so that through learning and feeling what we are not, we could recognize and remember who we truly are. By looking at others around us, we can remember the One within the many. Through knowing and becoming intimate with our own darkness, we can open up to and reclaim our light.

This system was intentionally designed by the Source with perfect clarity. Just as the Source expresses itself through the polarities, so too does it express itself through the intentionality of its design. The polarities themselves are a part of the design, just as you yourself are.

Look for a moment at the world around you. Consider the innate natural order that pervades all of creation: the sun rises in the east of its own accord every day and sets in the west. Earth rotates on its axis continuously, bringing us closer to and then farther away from the sun, thereby creating the four seasons. The waters of the rivers and oceans ebb and flow with the inherent intelligence of the tides. Animals instinctually know when it is time to hunt, to migrate, and to hibernate. The same inherent intelligence that governs creation also stirs within you. You may recognize it as the whisper of your higher self or your intuitive guidance, gently beckoning you toward your highest good in all areas of your life.

The world around you is literally God's playground, of which every crevice of creation is imbued with the innate wisdom and intentionality of the Source. Like a great artist who deliberately selects precisely the particular materials needed to carry out his great vision, so did the great Creator carry out its vision with crystal clarity. In other words, the Source knew exactly what it was doing as it birthed creation into being.

This concept was made clear to me in the peak moment of my spiritual awakening experience, when I came face to face with the Source of Creation. In my heightened and awakened state, I experienced the Source as an all-powerful, all-consuming green light. There were no words for me to assign to my experience but instead just powerful and instantaneous revelations and sensations. One of the sensations that stood out most clearly to me, and one that I recalled for a long time after my experience, was that of the intentionality and consciousness of that which I had witnessed. Through my experience I understood that the Source knowingly and intentionally devised its creation. There were no random occurrences, no accidents, no unplanned corners left unturned. There is free will granted to all living beings, to be sure; but even the allocation of free will is by design.

The intentionality with which the Source created the world is known in perfect clarity within the Spirit World. It is known to each of us as well before we incarnate into our human bodies and our minds become so weighed down by the heavy influence of maya, or illusion, that exists around us. The denseness and fogginess of the Earth plane is the polarity to the lightness and crystal clarity that exists within the Spirit World. This same clarity exists within your own spirit. It simply takes a bit more effort and practice when incarnated into a body to access that clarity once again.

The denseness of the Earth plane and the murkiness of our egos have caused humanity to become confused about the true qualities of Source. Humanity has fallen into the trap of duality, thereby becoming divided in regard to what constitutes the true definition of God. Many of us have become so attached and addicted to the need to be right in our definition and understanding of the infinite that we have allowed the ego's constant desire to attach to a particular viewpoint to cloud our true perception, thereby losing the clarity that truly resides within our Spirits. In decades past we have succumbed to a punitive image of an authoritative Godhead that is both limiting and stifling in nature. This paradigm of divinity is so far removed from the all-pervasive truth of what Source actually is that it has led humanity into brutal and savage wars that justify acts of violence against one other.

In fact, the truth of what God is, is quite simple and can be broken down into just one quality: Love. The divine consciousness, which is rooted in Love, desired to expand and to know itself, thereby creating the appearance of polarities in the world so that human beings could know and recognize themselves through the other. This process of awakening and healing was set up to take place on the miraculous stage of the Earth and was devised intentionally with perfect clarity, with only the highest purpose for our collective healing, evolution, and growth.

Gazing around us, we are surrounded by the constant reminders of the Source at work. Darkness and light, night and day, warmth and cold, form and formlessness: all the polarities are engaged in a continuous dance with one another within the interplay of creation. They weave in and out, up and down, around and behind one another, not in a struggle for control and domination over the other but rather as equal partners that help to define one another. Their dance is as joyful as it is playful. Through this eternal dance, initiated into motion by the hands of the great Creator, all of the world comes alive.

May we learn to recognize the oneness that underlies all of the polarities so that ultimately we understand that the many are truly the one. Through this understanding, humanity can begin to embrace all of the many names of Source—whether it be Allah, Jehovah, Jesus, or Buddha—as different facets of the same infinite and eternal consciousness, which is rooted in Love.

PART TWO: FORM
ALLY SPEAKS

A NOTE FROM ALLY

It is with great love, humility, and compassion that I offer you the following words and teachings that flow through these pages. Even if we do not know each other—even if our individual paths never crossed in this lifetime—fear not, for we are nonetheless connected through an intricate web of divine creation that surpasses the mind's level of understanding. The fact that you are holding this book in your hands today shows that we are connected. Your heart and mind were meant to take in these words at this time.

The following words are an offering from my heart to yours. They are meant to serve as touchstones of learning and inspiration in your life. They are meant to point and guide you in the direction of your own heart and to mine the treasure that resides there. They are not meant to provide concrete answers, to tell you what you should think or believe, or to absolve you of the responsibility of seeking the truth that dwells within you.

In the following pages, I share lessons from the Spirit World that are highly relevant to the times you are living in now. Each topic has been carefully and intentionally chosen for the valuable lessons that it brings. Some of these concepts may be topics you are familiar with and some of them may be new to you. What I ask of you as you proceed to read these pages is to embark on this journey with an open heart and mind. Some of the topics I explore, such as reincarnation, soul groups, and twin flames may clash with traditional religious belief systems. Some of the topics may challenge old paradigms of belief and ask you to step into new ones. In these pages, I invite you to explore the territory of the unknown, for that is the only place where true growth can occur.

Ultimately the journey you take as you read this book is yours, as is your unique journey through life. I honor your experience and I am blessed to share this journey with you.

With everlasting love, Ally

THE JOURNEY OUT

Your soul is ready to return home.

You have embarked upon a grand adventure, and now it is time
to return. You have laughed, you have cried, you have grown
and shared and learned and lost your way only to find it again
in this matrix of your life on Earth. A grand journey it has been,
and now it is time to return to the place from which you came,
the place which is etched into the cellular remembrance of your
DNA. Your mind may not remember the joy of the Spirit World,
but your heart knows it well. There is nothing for you to fear, for
all that awaits you on the other side is the infinite and expanding
Love of creation.

As you walk through the veil that separates the Earth plane from
the Spirit World, fear not, beloved one; for your heart rejoices in
the sweetness of your homecoming, yet again.

INTRODUCTION

THE TRUTHS OF THE SOUL

Philosophical questions regarding the purpose of mankind's existence have been considered since the dawn of consciousness. It is time now, at the beginning of a new age of consciousness for humankind, to embrace the timeless knowledge and truth of the soul—that which has been accessible to humanity all along but is now simply making its way into awareness faster and more powerfully than ever before. These universal truths, which humankind needs desperately to remember, are like beacons of light that serve to end the suffering that is caused by fear of the unknown. Such truths are accessible to all human beings on the planet; indeed, they are the birthright of every man and woman on the Earth.

The time has come for mankind to fully accept these truths of the soul. They are merely principles and remembrances of which your heart and soul have known all along and which your mind has forgotten. Through finding the willingness to open up to such wisdom, you open up your heart to remembering your soul's own beauty and light. It is this state of remembrance that will shift humankind from a state of deprivation, darkness, and fear. In other words, remaining in a place of forgetfulness of our divinity will no longer work; it is time to bring in the light.

In order for this shift in consciousness to take root, every person must do their part. This does not require human beings to give up specific beliefs about religion or traditions that are dear to them. Quite conversely, this shift will inspire many people around the world to embrace new traditions that speak to their heart, possibly traditions to which they had been closed to before. There will be a reemergence of the old traditions of the past and a return to the Earth and the plant-based wisdom of traditions such as shamanism and paganism. Religious traditions that encourage people to tune in to the wisdom of their hearts and their bodies will be embraced, while religious traditions steeped in dogma, control, and hierarchy will become obsolete. There will be an increased desire for authenticity and unity within all spiritual practices.

These shifts only indicate the beginning ripple effects of the upcoming planetary changes. The shift in the collective consciousness of mankind will happen progressively and in stages. Rather than a linear process, the shift will be organic in nature and will affect different people in different ways. No one, however, will be exempt from the massive changes that are taking place at this time. It is truly a remarkable time to be embodied on the Earth. Human beings are on the leading edge of consciousness in a universe that is on the leading edge of expansion. It is like the rumblings of a great earthquake; some rumblings are minor and start slow, while some are large and cause massive damage of the infrastructure that was already in place. And while the destruction of the old buildings and infrastructure can feel frightening at first, it is clearing the path for better, stronger buildings to be erected in its place. The beauty and splendor of the buildings to come far outweigh the initial fear that can be felt as the original buildings come crumbling down.

This metaphor can be applied to the changes taking place on Earth at this time. It is imperative that humanity unite as a whole to ascend to the next level of consciousness. Without this sense of unity, humanity will not survive. These are the lessons that are to be learned in order to salvage both the human race and the planet. Human beings now are being called to rise up to a higher level of responsibility and consciousness than ever before. Everyone can, in their own way, contribute to the facilitation of this cosmic shift. Many souls are already heeding this call and are acutely aware of the changes that are underway. Those who are as of yet unaware will be greatly assisted by those who are choosing to make the expansion of consciousness their work. Awareness is key, and once you have awareness, there is no turning back. In this race, the only way out is *through.*

There are many young children who are being born at this time with the purpose and intention of contributing to this evolutionary shift. These apparently young souls are actually very old souls with deep wisdom and knowledge and many gifts to impart to the world. They will become the leaders of the next generation, who will usher humanity into its next stage of development.

Yet everyone, no matter what age, has an important role to play. Every man, woman, and child must do their part and contribute to this work, for it is truly the only work in which you are engaged. There is nothing else because everything ultimately relates back to this. The interconnectivity between human beings on Earth is increasing rapidly and shall continue to increase. Therefore the actions, intentions, and behavior of one person affect that of all people. Collectively, if human beings consciously learned to join their intentions and power together for the greater good, the result would be unstoppable.

The lessons and chapters that I have included here are designed to give you a blueprint of the lessons that your soul came to learn on the great school of Earth. They are designed to assist you in seeing the bigger picture of your existence as a human being and your soul's journey, as well as your innate creative power. They are also designed to help remove feelings of fear and insecurity and allow you to reclaim your natural state of wellness, creativity, and joy. The intention of this information is to help promote humanity's ascension into the next stage of human consciousness, for one person's awakening is an awakening for all.

Allow yourself to receive the full benefit of each lesson. Allow these lessons to speak to your heart, to your consciousness, and most of all to your soul. Reading this book is designed to be not a process of learning but rather a process of remembering, for all that you are about to read are beautiful gemstones of truth that your mind has forgotten but that your spirit has known all along.

CHAPTER SEVEN

THE SPIRIT WORLD: ITS INNATE ORCHESTRATION AND ORDER

There are as many interpretations and explanations of what the Spirit World is and looks like as there are human beings that populate the Earth. I am here to tell you that none of them are true and all of them are true. Each one of them captures a small essence or nugget of the larger truth, which is beyond the totality and grasp of the mind. The human mind is capable of comprehending only a tiny fraction of the truth and oneness that the spiritual plane *is*, and what it is able to comprehend, it does through the lens of its ingrained perceptions and judgments of reality. Because human beings operate from the perspective of duality on the Earth plane—seeing things as good or bad, right or wrong, helpful or unhelpful—this is naturally the same lens with which humans attempt to understand the nonphysical realms. This attempt, however, can never succeed, because the basic operating principles of the spiritual world are completely different. It is like taking off glasses with your correct prescription and exchanging them for glasses with a completely different prescription—and then expecting to find your way around and see easily. It just will not work.

To truly understand the nature of the spiritual realm while still in an earthly body, one must see beyond the normal limitations of the mind. The easiest and most attainable way to do this is through meditation. Other methods will include ways of achieving an altered state of consciousness, such as hypnosis, shamanic rituals, and various healing modalities and energy work. Again, there are as many methods available as there are human beings to practice them.

You should not despair or feel discouraged at the mind's inability to comprehend infinity. Indeed, rest assured that this natural limitation of the mind was set up intentionally. In your human body, you are not meant to grasp the totality of your being and all of creation. On the contrary, you are meant to forget. This is the way in which the system of creation operates, and it is established this way for a reason. Do not ever doubt this. If nothing else, the Spirit World is orchestrated and ordered with such a high degree of intentionality that there is nothing that parallels this same level of orchestration on the Earth plane—although, of course, the Earth plane operates on its own level of order and harmony as well.

The difference is that the density of the Earth often prevents the flow from running smoothly. Things can and do become stuck more easily on Earth. On the Earth plane, there are barriers that block the flow of the innate harmony of the universe and the energetic flow within yourself. Such barriers are always present for a reason, yet that reason can become easily obscured in the density of the Earth. In the higher frequencies of the Spirit World, such blocks do not exist. There is complete clarity and flow at all times. It is like a glorious, choreographed dance in which all elements and parts correspond seamlessly.

Although this seamless flow of the Spirit World is not as present on the Earth plane, in the deepest recesses of your being, you can and do remember the experience of such orchestration. It is not a knowing that is contained within your conscious or even your subconscious or unconscious memory. It exists deeper than that, within the warehouse of the superconscious memory of your soul. This remembrance informs and influences you throughout your life in your earthly body.

Every soul, without exception, is encoded with the remembrance of its true identity and home of the Spirit World. The degree to which souls can access this remembrance and are open to delving into it is the differentiating factor. I want to assure you that there is no way a soul could not harbor the innate knowledge of its true nature and true home. It is simply not possible, because that truth is one with who you are. Even the most proclaimed atheist or skeptic harbors this knowledge inside him or her. This remembrance transcends religion; in fact, it is completely unrelated to religion of any kind. This remembrance signifies the soul's recognition of itself as consciousness. It is the spark that ignites the recognition of the eternal, undying spirit manifested in physical form. In many traditions this spark of recognition has been called awakening.

Remembrance of the Spirit World is innate and completely natural to you. You can and do have access to all of the information that you seek about the Spirit World. It is all inside of you and has been since the day you were born. In many cases this information is buried deep below the surface level of awareness. If your ordinary conscious mind is the top layer of an ocean, then this information is stored at the deepest crevasses of the bottom of the ocean. Yet it is not inaccessible. Of course there is a reason for this information to be so hidden, and there is great value as well in remembering and attaining this information once again. After all, what point is there in the journey if you do not have anything to seek or anywhere to go?

The entirety of your consciousness is more complex and vast than you could imagine. There is no scientist, nor any scientific procedure, that could begin to capture and explain the mystery of your being. It is completely beyond the grasp of the mind, and while incarnated into a human body, it is oftentimes difficult to grasp the magnificence and orchestration of your own consciousness.

Your mind is like a giant warehouse with many levels. The first level of the warehouse represents ordinary consciousness, in which the mind produces thoughts, emotions, and judgments ceaselessly. These thought forms operate in a transient fashion, coming into your awareness and then leaving again. Most people tend to spend many lifetimes and much of their current lives focused on the first floor of the warehouse.

The second and third floors represent deeper layers of consciousness. This could be referred to as the subconscious and unconscious parts of the mind. These are the layers that begin to penetrate deeper beneath the transient thought-forms and deeper into the beingness beyond your mind. As each floor progresses, it becomes necessary to use various methods to access that floor. For instance, you may gain access to the second floor of the warehouse through meditation and access to the third floor through hypnosis. Once access has been granted and you have visited a particular floor of the warehouse of your mind, it becomes easier to travel there again a second or third or fourth time.

The number of floors in the warehouse of your mind is infinite. There is no finite number of floors. They continue ascending higher and higher—or, rather, deeper and deeper—into your being. Each floor brings you closer to your true nature as consciousness and further from your identification with this body and mind. It is important to understand that there is no final ending place. Human souls are engaged in a continual process of deepening that never ends. In fact, the journey continues once a soul leaves its human body. In the Spirit World, there is continual learning and evolution as well as lessons to be learned. Lifetime after lifetime, you journey into a new human body, each time exploring different portions of the warehouse of your mind. It is an ongoing journey of self-discovery that always serves to bring you back to the place you were all along.

Understanding the orchestration and depth of the Spirit World benefits you greatly because it impacts your perspective while living on Earth. When you are able to grasp even a slight understanding of the vastness of your mind, the eternal nature of your spirit, and the intentionality of the world beyond the physical one, you enrich your experience in this physical human body. Understanding that your spirit is undying and that your soul will continue on its journey, even after the demise of the physical body, serves as a tremendous relief to many. This knowledge relieves the immense fear of death that many souls feel throughout their many lifetimes. Knowledge of the innate order of the Spirit World also serves as a comfort to souls who question the purpose and mechanism of the universe.

CHAPTER EIGHT

THE IMPORTANCE OF INNER HARMONY AND ALIGNMENT

I t is of utmost importance that you learn to find inner harmony and alignment in your life while in your physical body. This intention exceeds all others in importance. It is greater than that of achieving financial success, of finding a mate, of buying material things, of anything you could ever do, possess, or have while on planet Earth. This is because all the things that you seek and desire most in the world flow from the space of inner harmony and alignment within yourself. It is much like creating the foundation of a house or a building. In order for the house to be stable and successful, it must have the appropriate grounding beneath it to support its evolution and growth.

You are that house. That is, in your earthly body, you are the one who is creating all the success and desires that you seek. You are constantly co-creating with your environment in an ongoing process through your thoughts, words, actions, and intentions. When you do not feel proper alignment within yourself, however, your energy becomes blocked, and it cannot flow in the way that it is innately meant to. It is like building a great dam in a river; a lack of inner harmony stops the flow of the water. So it is within yourself as well.

What often happens is that many souls become distracted by the excitement and charm of their external world. Souls become enticed by the people, circumstances, relationships, pleasures, and experiences of the environment around them. Basically, souls become distracted by the "game." In their distraction, they place greater emphasis on their external surroundings than they do their internal experience. They focus outward rather than inward and therefore neglect to pay attention to the barometer of their own inner alignment. Their inner alignment becomes askew, and their outer world cannot help but follow because the inner and outer worlds are completely one.

In other words, the outer world around you is nothing but a mirror reflection of your internal world. To souls in physical bodies, it may not seem that this is so. Many souls forget this truth and assume that the outer world has no relation to their inner experience, but this could not be further from the truth. The veils of separation do not exist. This is a truth that many souls have forgotten, and as a result the inhabitants of Earth are paying a dear price.

When you change your internal world, you automatically change your outer world as well. If, for instance, you begin to practice positive self-talk and speak more kindly to yourself on a consistent basis, you will begin to notice that others around you begin to speak more kindly to you as well. This occurrence may surprise you, yet what has truly changed? Was it the people around you who suddenly became more kind? No, it was the result of you internally shifting your inner world, which in turn shifted the outer reality around you. This and a million other examples confirm the synchronicity of the inner and outer realms.

Finding inner harmony and alignment are the keys to unlocking the doors and the vastness of the universe. Ultimately, what is meant by inner harmony and alignment is simply finding a state of peace within yourself. It should be understood that this state is your natural default. You are naturally aligned. You are naturally peaceful. You are naturally harmonious with everyone and everything in your environment at all times. This is your true resting state. It is only the judgments and fluctuations of the mind, as well as false negative beliefs and fears created by the ego, that detract from this natural and peaceful resting place.

Many of these beliefs and fears are learned in childhood, and many others develop over time. It is the mission and work of the human experience to begin and continue the process of unraveling these limiting perceptions, some of which have persisted for multiple lifetimes. It is a continual, ongoing process of self-discovery that never ends but only takes you deeper and closer to the truth. The more you are engaged in removing the layers of falsity that cloak your being, the more your true inner alignment and harmony can shine through. You will never fully arrive at a place where you are done seeking alignment, either in this life or in the next, for the exploration of your inner harmony is infinite. In other words, you are seeking harmony with your spirit while in physical form, and your consciousness will never fully meet itself. It does not ever get to a place of arrival where it is finished. You may imagine your purpose and evolution as a soul to be a continual dance of becoming rather than attempting to arrive at any final destination. The joy is found in the dance itself rather than in the final execution.

Even while in your physical body, your spirit knows and understands what inner harmony and alignment feel like. You may experience this feeling when you are somewhere beautiful in nature. Or you may experience it when you are spending time with close family or friends whom you love. You may feel inner harmony when you are engaged in doing something that you are passionate about, like a sport or hobby. Almost all souls can identify what this inner alignment feels like in some capacity.

Your mission is to begin to cultivate this state of inner harmony more often than not. This can happen in many ways, and the process will differ for each individual. For some people it may look like beginning to cultivate new, positive thought patterns about themselves and the world around them. For others, it may involve spending more time engaged in activities that bring them to a state of inner peace. For others still it may look like making drastic life changes, such as shifting out of a job or a relationship that is preventing the person from finding inner alignment. All of these are valid methods of seeking inner harmony. The process will look different for each soul, and some souls may progress more quickly than others. This, too, is as it should be. There is no race to the finish line, after all. There are only deeper layers of understanding and joy that are reached as each soul continues its journey in its perfect time and pace.

When you learn to prioritize your inner alignment over everyone and everything else, you will watch in wonderment as things in your life begin to unfold. There is not a more powerful way to create drastic changes in your life than by shifting your internal environment and returning to the natural state of peace, equanimity, and bliss that is your birthright and your true nature. Although it may take some souls years or even lifetimes to reclaim this natural state of being, every soul will eventually return to its original state of grace and purity.

CHAPTER NINE

FORGIVENESS OF SELF
AND OTHERS

O ne of the greatest spiritual lessons that souls must master is that of forgiveness. The vibration of forgiveness is such that it releases stuck and stagnant energy from the etheric body. Many souls, however, experience difficulty in fully integrating this lesson, both while in the physical body on Earth and as a soul in the Spirit World. This difficulty arises from attachment to ego. It is the human ego that is resistant to forgiveness. There are many reasons for this, such as the need or desire to be right, fear of being wrong and being judged, fear of opening the heart, and the desire to remain angry versus opening up to vulnerability. The reasons for lack of forgiveness are as vast and varied as the souls who harbor anger or resentment for various perceived grievances.

Cultivating the energy of forgiveness creates freedom. There is great energy contained in the vibration of anger, bitterness, and resentment. In other words, it requires large amounts of energy to sustain such emotions within the mind and the body. Forgiveness is the key to unlocking this stagnant energy and setting it free. A soul cannot truly be free to advance on its spiritual journey without mastering the art of forgiveness. A soul cannot experience freedom if it is harboring anger and resistance over a particular situation, regardless of how long ago the situation occurred. Actually, the older a particular situation is that has yet to be forgiven, the more energy is required to sustain the vibration of resistance and anger. It is far easier to release energy over more recent situations than it is older ones. You may think of it like old scar tissue; the older the injury is, the more time it has had to ingrain itself into the skin and tissues, and the longer it will take to heal.

This is why it is vitally important to release the energy of anger and resentment as soon as it arises, rather than allowing it to build and gain more energy. There is a tendency of the human ego to label such emotions as bad, which in turn causes reluctance in many souls to directly address and discuss the circumstances creating those emotions. Suppression of anger is never helpful and causes much more harm than good. It is always better to confront the precipitating factors of the anger than to ignore them and brush them to the side, which in fact only gives more power and energy to the emotions. "What you resist persists" is an accurate description of this process. If, for example, a person who experiences anger at being treated unfairly with his or her boss decides to repress those feelings rather than expressing them respectfully, the energy that is harnessed to create that repression will act like a magnet that serves to attract more feelings of anger and resentment into that person's life. This is a basic law of the universe and is true without exception.

The more you can allow yourself to express and release feelings of anger, disappointment, resentment, or any other emotion that blocks the energy of forgiveness, the more freedom you will create within your own being and soul. Forgiveness is the antidote to nearly all of the pains of humanity. When you allow yourself to forgive someone in your own life, that act of forgiveness impacts the collective consciousness of all human beings everywhere. The act of forgiveness sends out a vibration into the world that resonates at a higher frequency than that of greed, anger, fear, or vengefulness.

It is the single most healing thing you can do for yourself and for other people in the world.

One of the most significant lessons in forgiveness is about learning to forgive yourself. Most souls, for one reason or another, learn to judge themselves extremely harshly. The harshness and critical nature with which souls tend to judge themselves is much more harmful in nature than any judgment that is ever passed on human souls from the more highly evolved beings and guides. In other words, human beings tend to judge themselves much more critically than other beings in the Spirit Realm. In fact, there is no judgment at all from higher guides. There is only a sense of unconditional love, acceptance, and compassion of each soul's journey and lessons. There is a deep acknowledgment and understanding of the karmic lessons and experiences that each soul has chosen to address in their lives. Guides who reside in the Spirit Realm have the capacity to instantaneously glimpse the entirety of a particular soul's life span, purpose, and journey. Therefore, there exists nothing of criticism, judgment, or condemnation from the higher beings in the Spirit Realm. Such beings desire nothing more than to witness and rejoice in a particular soul's triumphs and successful learning process.

Many souls incarnate repeatedly throughout a span of many lives in order to release anger in regard to a particular person or situation. If the intended learning does not occur in a given lifetime, that soul will inevitably return again in another life, with a different story and location and circumstance, but with the same karmic lesson. Forgiveness that is not attained in one lifetime will thus return in another, but the second, third, or fourth time around, the lessons are likely to be more difficult and painful. This is not the result of universal punitive or spiteful action but a learning tactic that is initiated in order to gain that soul's attention. If, for example, a man in his late forties is unable to forgive his wife for cheating on him and retaliates against her by treating her poorly, and if he chooses to hold on to that anger and bitterness

101

for the rest of his life, he will most certainly reincarnate again with that particular soul in a different time and space. This time, instead of his wife cheating on him, he may experience a scenario in which his spouse or child steals from him, abandons him, or causes him emotional or physical harm in some way. The same story will unfold with different scenery and characters. The play will continue on until the karmic lessons have been learned and balanced.

There is no inherent judgment in the establishment of reincarnation. In other words, it is not bad or unfair or wrong if a soul must reincarnate again in order to learn appropriate lessons of forgiveness. (There are many other lessons that souls are working toward learning, of course, but forgiveness is one of the most common and significant lessons.) In fact, it is quite natural and appropriate that this be the cycle of learning. The cycle of reincarnation is divinely guided and is as inherent and natural to humankind as is the cycle of breathing. It is the way in which human beings evolve spiritually and develop as souls. There is deep order and brilliance in the orchestration of this cycle. Most souls, with very few exceptions, do indeed need to reincarnate multiple times to return to the "Earth school" and learn their soul lessons. There is no better way for souls to learn lessons of forgiveness, acceptance, and compassion than by gaining a physical body and engaging on planet Earth.

The more a soul can practice lessons of forgiveness in his or her everyday life, the more that soul will accelerate the rate of his or her spiritual growth. There is no race, of course, and learning to practice forgiveness is beneficial not only to the person practicing it but to everyone involved in the situation. On a broader scale, practicing forgiveness benefits all of humankind as well. The acts of forgiveness need not be drastic in nature. They may be as simple as deciding to forgive someone who cuts you off in line at the grocery store or while driving in traffic. It may be an act as seemingly inconsequential as forgiving someone who bumps into you at a store or speaks rudely to you on the phone. Rest assured that every act of forgiveness, no matter how small, is never inconsequential. Conversely, each incident that occurs that causes you to harbor resentment or anger, no matter how trivial, is like collecting a small pebble of coal that germinates inside your body and mind. Over time, unless you practice the act of forgiveness, those small coals begin to build up and cause internal damage. Practicing forgiveness is the antidote to this damage. It is much like housecleaning, because it serves to sweep away the grime that has been collected from days, months, or years of built-up resentment and tension.

There are many ways in which to practice and facilitate forgiveness, and none are better than the others. The methods of practicing forgiveness are as vast and widespread as the people who practice them. Some of these methods may include meditating, praying, talking directly to a person, addressing a difficult situation, writing a letter, or journaling. The gesture does not need to be drastic in order for it to be effective. When practicing forgiveness, you will know whether the practice has been effective or not by the way that you feel. If you experience a lightness in your being, increased energy, lack of resistance, or feelings of peacefulness and acceptance, then the practice has been effective. On the other hand, if after the practice, you continue to feel heaviness or feelings of anger or bitterness, then that is an indication that the practice was ineffective. If this is the case, all that is indicated is a shift in the approach. Practicing forgiveness is much more an art form than it is a structured formula.

Continue to work toward forgiveness in all of your interactions, big and small. Allow yourself to find the joy in this process. This is the soul work that you agreed to undertake as you embarked upon this journey upon the school of Earth. There is no greater work than this.

CHAPTER TEN

LISTENING

There is no greater art than that of listening. It is an art and a science because there is both discernment and consideration, as well as great skill, involved in the act of listening. It is a skill that is highly underdeveloped in the general population at this time. There are many reasons for this, including underappreciation for the process of being in stillness and quiet, and an increased emphasis on generating action and noise.

There are multiple sources of distractions in the world today. The world is becoming increasingly noisy, and the ascension of technology is contributing to this. Technology and noise are not by themselves bad, but they can prevent the opportunity for deeper connection to occur. Underneath the noise exists the space that contains it. Unless we develop an awareness of the space and quiet that permeate all things, the noise around us become meaningless chatter without any real value.

The act of listening is not the linear, simplified act that it is often understood to be. There is in fact a great deal of complexity involved in listening, as there are many ways in which to listen. For the purposes of our discussion, we will explore the two most relevant types of listening: *inner* and *outer* listening.

Outer listening is the type of listening that most people typically use. This type of listening involves active engagement with people in the world around you. Even in this type of listening, there are many different layers involved. For example, you may listen to teachers in classrooms at school. You may listen to friends, coworkers, family members, and your spouse when they talk to you. You listen to strangers when they introduce themselves to you.

But the type of listening I am referring to is not merely hearing the words that are being said and spoken. On a deeper level, listening refers to hearing what is being left unsaid as much as to hearing what is being said. Body language and verbal cues have much to do with this. On an even deeper level is feeling into the underlying vibration and energy beneath the words that are being expressed. This is what true outer listening implies. It is not just an active state of listening to the words a person is saying but also involves engaging in a *feeling* state of receptivity in which you allow yourself to tap into the vibration of the words that are uttered.

For example, you may use outer listening during a conversation with your mother in which she tells you that she is upset with you because you missed her phone call. Her tone of voice and body language may convey to you that she is feeling angry, yet the energy and vibration beneath her words suggest a deeper, underlying emotion of hurt. If you had only listened to her actual words rather than tuning into her underlying vibrational state, then you would not have gleaned this insightful information.

There is always an underlying vibration beneath the words that are being spoken. Everyone and everything around you is composed of vibration, and conversations and words are no exception. The more you can begin to attune yourself to the vibrations of the people around you, the more you will begin to truly hear what is being said, as well as what is not being said.

With practice, you will be able to pause and ask yourself, "Is this person coming from a vibration of love or fear? What energy pattern is present beneath the words that I am hearing? What vibrational pattern is being formed by these sentences and words?"

Your words are your most powerful tool, and everyone around you is using this tool as well. Your words are the building blocks of your reality. The words you speak begin to morph the unmanifest—the world of vibration and sound—into tangible reality. Thus it is crucial for you to begin to properly understand and use this remarkable ability with discernment and awareness.

It will likely take some practice to get accustomed to listening in this way. It is not the manner in which you are taught to listen, and it may take some time to begin shifting your perspective on listening and how it is done. Your intention to listen on a deeper level to those around you is all that is needed for you to begin to make this shift. It is actually quite simple. What makes the process difficult is the ego's resistance to being present enough to listen to another person.

True listening requires great presence. Indeed, true listening and presence are, in fact, one and the same. You cannot listen to another person if you cannot slow your mind down enough to focus on them and what they are saying. You cannot create enough space in your own mind to receive their words if your mind is so cluttered by your thoughts that there is nowhere for the information to go. To really listen to someone, you must be fully present and engaged in the moment. There is no other way.

This type of presence and mindfulness is the segue to the second type of listening, which I will call inner listening. Unlike outer listening, in which attention is directed outward, this type of listening implies a deep turning inward. It requires a willingness to sit and be present *with oneself.* It requires the strength to sit and simply be. Generally this is not an easy task for souls to do, particularly in this current time. There are many, many distractions and stimulations available to people in this age, ranging from television to social events to the internet to various mind-altering substances.

More than anything, the human ego fears facing itself. It will therefore create distractions whenever it can. While some of these distractions can seem plausible at the time, they always serve as a smoke screen to cover up the fear and uneasiness that lie just beneath the surface level of awareness. The only way to release the fear is to learn to sit and become present with one's own inner being.

Learning to listen to your inner being is the true foundation for all success. All success and all that you desire in your human existence arises from this point. It cannot be found by focusing only outward; you must be willing to venture deep inside of yourself. There you will find an ocean of treasure and all the answers that you seek.

You do not need to learn to do this all at once but may progress in small steps. Some souls will find this easier to do than others. For some souls it is more natural to tune inward and engage in the inner world. For souls who are more externally driven, this process may feel unfamiliar or even uncomfortable. Yet this type of inner listening is easily accessible to all human beings, regardless of prior experience or personality type. It is a practice with which all humans are familiar on some level. It only needs to be reawakened within you.

There are many methods with which to awaken this inner listening. Each soul will have a different way that is most in alignment with their needs. Some souls may be able to access inner listening through meditation; others through movement, such as running or yoga; others through playing a musical instrument or making art; and others through time spent in nature. The method you use to tune into your inner being matters not compared to the quality and strength of the inner connection that you establish.

You may think of it as essentially plugging a giant cord directly from your own heart into universal consciousness. When you are plugged in to universal consciousness—which is accessible to all beings at all times—you are, in fact, also plugged in to your own inner being, or your own soul, if you will. In fact, it is impossible for you to connect with universal consciousness without first establishing a connection with your own inner being. Why? Because they are one in the same. You were created from the universal Source and cannot separate yourself from it. It is impossible. So when you create the time and space in your life to *listen* within to the ringing that resounds from the core of your heart, you are also tapping into the Source from which you were born. Tapping into the Source tunes you into your own inner being; tapping into your own inner being tunes you into the Source, for they are one.

There is no equivalent to the wisdom and richness that you will find when you allow yourself to truly listen within. For some souls this is a truly terrifying experience, because they have been so conditioned to look outside of themselves for guidance and answers. It can also be quite unsettling for souls to listen and look within themselves because they feel so uncomfortable being with themselves. Both of these objections are resistances of the ego, and both relate to the same basic, underlying fear: that deep down, we are not good enough; that we are unworthy; that we are unlovable; that, therefore, we cannot trust what we hear within, because it is not safe or okay to do so. Whatever variations (and there are many), that fear may take, it ultimately leads to the same place: that it is not safe to listen within and to experience the *being* with oneself that inner listening demands.

Learning to listen within and to be with yourself in this process is a great act of self-love. It is an immense act of self-love because through your attentive listening and presence, you are acknowledging that you are worth listening to. You are also sending yourself the message that it is safe to trust your own inner knowing. Simply put, through your listening, you are being present with yourself and to yourself. It is a process of holding yourself without judgment and being present to whatever arises from within.

You're feeling angry or irritated? Listen to that feeling. Your mind keeps replaying an incident that happened with your friend the day previously? Listen to why that scenario continues to unfold in your consciousness. You're feeling a sense of serenity and peace? Listen to those emotions, and allow them to inform you of the state of your inner being. You are not trying to change any-thing—no, that is not the point. When a good friend calls you in a state of heightened emotion and says they need to just vent, what do you do? You allow them to express their thoughts and feelings while you just listen. That is precisely what this process is like, ex-cept that it is directed within instead of without.

The more that you can begin to practice listening to yourself in this way, the more connected and aligned with your inner being you will be. It will not only heighten your awareness but will enrich every aspect of your life experience, for as you learn to listen more deeply to others around you, so, too, will you be able to listen more deeply within to the stirring of your own consciousness and your own heart. In actuality, there is no real division between outer listening and inner listening, for they are both but extensions of the same process, just being pointed in different directions. In this sense, listening to one person is listening to all people, and listen-ing to yourself is listening to the cries, hopes, and dreams of the whole planet and all the beings that dance upon it.

Listen. Can you hear?

CHAPTER ELEVEN

SOUL GROUPS

All human souls, prior to the time of their incarnation, exist within soul groups. These groups are like different clusters, or neighborhoods, of souls that are organized according to different soul-learning levels. It is much like a giant classroom on the other side of the veil. This is part of the orchestration and order of the Spirit World. Not all spirits dwell in this classroom, either because they have graduated and it no longer fulfills a purpose for them or because they have chosen to participate in systems of reality other than the three-dimensional Earth plane. Even so, however, those spirits will still be focused and oriented in a training ground of their own to best suit their unique needs.

Much information is available now in regard to the concept of soul groups and twin flames. This is not a bad thing; indeed, it indicates the degree to which the veil is thinning. Yet because of the vastness of information available, it is important to gain information that is accurate, accessible, applicable, and relatable. It is my intention here to provide some of the clearest information available today.

Souls incarnate in soul groups. There is no set finite number for how many souls can dwell in a soul group, although that number is usually determined by the level of advancement of the souls in the group. For instance, younger souls typically require more individual attention from guides, and therefore groups of younger souls tend to be smaller. Groups of advanced souls typically require less individualized attention and so may be larger, but there is no hard-and-fast rule. The exact number of souls in a soul group is the appropriate number for that group. The structure of the group is handled by the senior guides who overlook the overall progress and advancement of each individual soul as well as the group as a whole.

The souls who are together in a soul group share a deep and intimate connection that transcends linear time. These souls have journeyed and shared many incarnations together on the Earth plane. This does not necessarily imply that the roles taken by each soul in each other's lives was a pleasant one. In fact, some of the soul relationships carried out on the Earth plane may have been especially painful or difficult. For instance, a mother and son who experienced difficulty and animosity in their relationship on Earth would still be within the same soul group in the Spirit World. In other words, the degree of amicability in relationship with someone in an Earth life does not correspond to whether or not a soul is in a person's soul group.

In fact, if there is someone in your life with whom you have a particularly painful relationship, or someone in your life who has abandoned you physically or through death, it is likely that you are in the same soul group with that person. This may seem counterintuitive and yet makes sense when you consider the degree of commitment, love, and sacrifice required to willingly take on a difficult role in the life of someone you care about. The people who come into your life to teach you the most difficult soul lessons are the ones who care about you deeply, so deeply that they are willing to play a role in your life that causes you pain because they know it will provide a necessary lesson for advancement on a soul level.

It can be difficult, if not downright painful, to acknowledge this type of divine orchestration, for we are often taught to believe that a loving God would not and should not allow painful events to happen in our lives. We may ask ourselves, *How can an all-loving God allow this to happen?* Yet think about it: When were the times in your life when you learned and grew the most from your life experiences? Was it during the times when everything was going well? Or was it during the times when you were struggling, when you were moving through something challenging, that you received the most wisdom from your experiences? In most cases, it is the latter, for the painful experiences in our lives—whether it be a difficult relationship, losing a job, or the loss of someone you love—hold the most potential to catapult us forward into the next phase of our growth and evolution on a soul level. Your spirit harbors an understanding of this truth and is aware of its guiding orchestration in the Spirit World. That is why other souls within your soul group frequently agree to play "difficult" roles in your life on Earth and why they may agree to carry out certain actions that are difficult for you to experience—because on a soul level, they understand the higher function of these actions: to give you the opportunity to evolve and to learn the karmic lessons your soul came here to learn. From this perspective, it is truly an act of the highest service and love.

All of the souls within your soul group have been with you before. They are the souls with whom you incarnate repeatedly throughout time. Generally, they are the souls with whom you have evolved throughout your spiritual progression and evolution. They are your parents, friends, teachers, romantic partners, children, and loved ones. They are those with whom you reincarnate in order to resolve and clear karma, whether it be on an individual level or on a family level. There is not a hard-and-fast rule that the particular souls in a group can't fluctuate, but this only happens when it is truly deemed necessary by the senior guides. A soul may leave a particular group when, for example, that soul has progressed in its learning and evolution to such an extent that it requires more stimulation than what the current group can offer.

A soul might also leave its group when that soul is displaying great difficulty in meeting its learning objectives in its current group and is deemed to require a shift in energy that comes from joining another soul group. Instances such as this are relatively rare, however. The senior guides take great care to ensure that each soul is progressing forward in its life assignments and within its soul group.

There is great love present between members of a soul group. Between souls there exists an immediate and instant recognition of one another that transcends words. Indeed, there are no words in the Spirit World. Souls communicate by using telepathy, which occurs when there is a transfer of information within the minds of two souls. Human beings on the Earth plane have the ability to use telepathy as well, although most humans have forgotten that this is so.

This instant sense of knowing and love is the bond that glues soul groups together. All souls within a soul group know one another on a deep level. Unlike in the physical world, there is no hiding, no deceit, and no insecurity that can occur between members. All of the defenses of the ego are stripped away in the Spirit World, and indeed within the soul groups, there is no need for them. There is a consistent understanding from all members of the soul group about the lessons, issues, and strengths that a particular soul is working on in its spiritual development. For instance, members of a soul group would recognize that Solina, a soul who incarnated as a Japanese woman in her most recent life, was working through feelings of isolation and abandonment that had plagued her for lifetimes. At the same time, members would know Solina exhibited great strength of character in her devotion to living a pure and pious life. So you see, both the challenges and strengths are known to all, and there is no judgment, because no one is comparing themselves to anyone else. Everyone is on their unique journey, and it is unfolding in precisely the way it is meant to for that soul. Issues and hindrances of the mind, such as judgment, expectation, and comparison have no place in the Spirit World. Generally speaking, there is only a deep sense of clarity and acceptance concerning the life path of self and others.

Souls exist within groups for the purpose of supporting, uplifting, and serving one another. Souls could hardly expect to move forward spiritually without being in relationship with other souls. Each soul, prior to its incarnation, has different learning objectives that it outlines with its guide. Part of the reason that souls are delineated into groups is for the mutual support, encouragement, and upliftment that each soul receives from the others in regards to their personal karmic lessons and learning objectives. Just like in the physical world, souls benefit immensely from the mutual learning that takes place within the group, as well as the sense of comradery and connection that is gained from the group structure. Although each soul is on its individual and unique journey of growth, the benefit that souls receive from learning with one another in this fashion is truly immeasurable.

CHAPTER TWELVE

TWIN FLAMES AND SOUL MATES

There is a large amount of information available today on the topics of soul mates and twin flames. Some of this information is accurate, and some of it is not. Because of the misunderstanding regarding the intention and purpose of these types of soul relationships, there are some widely held misconceptions about what twin flames and soul mates really are. The information presented in this chapter will attempt to clarify and discern the truth regarding these different kinds of soul connections.

Souls cultivate deep relationships with one another through many lifetimes. Those in the same soul group reincarnate with one another countless times, each time taking on a different role in one another's lives according to the particular learning objectives and needs of that lifetime. A husband and wife in this life could have a long history of incarnating with one another as brothers, sisters, parent and child, or best friends. Over time, as these soul relationships deepen, they may begin to develop into other levels of soul relationships, such as those of soul mates and twin flames.

We will begin by looking at twin flames. The most common misconception regarding twin flames is that the term automatically implies a romantic relationship. This is not the case. Two people do not have to be romantically involved to be twin flames;

indeed, oftentimes they are not romantically involved, yet because of their limited understanding of what twin flames are, they do not recognize themselves as such.

The truth is that twin flames can be and often are friends, co-workers, business partners, parent and child, or sibling pairs. All of these relationships can involve a twin flame connection. "Twin flames" simply implies a relationship between two or more people in which there is a deep soul connection as well as the incentive to carry out work together that is for the greatest good of themselves and the planet. This is the main and most significant aspect of any twin flame relationship. In fact, the nature of the relationship matters less than the depth of the soul connection and the intention of the work to be carried out together.

Another common misconception regarding twin flames is that, because of the notion of "twins," there can only be two souls within the relationship. This is not the case. The notion of "twins" within the context of twin flames transcends our typical understanding of what twins are. Within twin flame relationships, the definition of twins is not focused on a twin relationship between two people. Rather, the term "twin" refers to the similarity and alignment of the work that is to be completed by these souls. Therefore, there may be three, four, or even five twin souls working together in an incarnation, although usually there are not more than three or four souls incarnated as twin souls at one time. In some instances there might be, although this is rare. More often, when there are higher numbers of twin souls working together, some souls are embodied and some are not. It is possible for a person to have a twin flame who has passed on or is even someone they have never met in this lifetime.

Regardless of the particular setup, twin flames are always those souls who share a combined higher purpose in the world. It is more of a partnership than it is a love relationship between two souls, although there often is great love involved in twin flame relationships. Therefore, twin flames could be business partners who work together to share a common mission or goal; they could be two people who, for most of their lives, didn't know each other until they were brought together by a certain passion or cause; or they could be two people around the world who have never met who are called to do some work in the world and are guided by the same ideals, values, and principles. Regardless of their external circumstances and environment, twin flame relationships always indicate a deep intimacy and closeness on the soul level. Even if two people who are twin flames live halfway around the world from each other and do not know each other, they undoubtedly do recognize each other on a soul level and have likely shared many past lives together.

It can be more complex than this, however. Looking outside of our linear definitions of time and space, twin flames can coexist within different levels of reality and in different dimensions. One counterpart of a twin flame relationship may live in fifteenth-century France as a Catholic priest, and the other counterpart may live in modern Southeast Asia in a small village as a monk. On the outside it would seem that there is little to no connection between these two souls, who live in entirely different parts of the world and in completely different time periods. These twin flame souls may have set up their relationship in precisely this way before they incarnated for certain reasons. For example, this twin soul pair may have decided that because in past incarnations they had spent a majority of their lives occupying the same time and space, it would be beneficial for them to incarnate in different countries and time periods. Despite their differing existences, however, they likely created an agreement to carry out similar missions in their respective lives. They may have both decided to devote their life's work to the God of their individual religion or to serve others through their religious beliefs. Although these twin flame souls are not aware of one another on a conscious level, on a soul level, they are completely aware of one another and of the agreement they created together before they incarnated. There is always a reason for twin flames to incarnate and work together. This reason is *always* aligned with the highest order and good of the universe. It is always work that must be done for the highest good of humanity and is imperative for the time period it is operating within. The work could not be done by one soul alone; it can only be done with both souls working together as a team.

In the case of the French Catholic priest and the Asian monk, these souls drew psychic energy from one another across time and space. They likely communicated often in dream states and were acting throughout their lives from an unconscious awareness of the plan they had created together before they incarnated. So even though these two individual souls did not know each other consciously and even existed in quite different realities from one another, they still could not have carried out the work they both needed to do without each other. This is a crucial point to understand. It is difficult to comprehend because it goes against conventional definitions of time and space. Such definitions are highly limited, however, and in reality they do not exist. Time, as we understand it, is a highly fluid, dynamic process that is not constricted at all. It only appears constricted through the lens of your human minds and bodies. That is why, in actuality, it is very possible for two souls to incarnate into lives where they have never even met one another physically and yet can still be twin souls. It can and does happen often.

Twin souls can even communicate through different layers of consciousness. That is what is happening in the case of this book. My sister, Purandev, is receiving information from me that I am bringing forth from the other side. This type of communication between twin souls happens often as well, yet frequently it is not recognized for what it truly is. For instance, someone who has experienced the death of a close friend or family member may find themselves creating beautiful works of art, or receiving guidance or intuition about a particular person or situation, or may begin to take a new direction in life that has great meaning for them and for others, such as volunteer work. This type of interaction is often generated by the deceased twin flame soul that has passed on. Seldom does the other twin flame consciously recognize the process that is occurring. It is not necessary for this recognition to be made, although it can bring greater comfort, relief, and understanding for those who are grieving.

It is important for people in the world to learn about the true nature of twin souls and all that it entails because it provides a deeper understanding of our eternal nature and our eternal connection to one another. Not everyone has a twin soul in this incarnation, but everyone has close relationships in their lives. Those who do not yet have a twin soul in this incarnation are working their way toward creating that partnership. Twin souls naturally imply a certain level of consciousness and evolution because the work that the twin souls carry out together is consciousness raising in nature. Therefore, those souls who are currently working on their first few incarnations will have a while to go before they develop and create their first twin flame relationship. That is well and as it should be, because each soul is exactly where it needs to be in its level of development. However, even those souls who have not yet manifested a twin flame relationship are sowing the seeds for that relationship today through their interactions, reactions, and relationships with others.

Twin souls have an important role to play in the continuing evolution of the planet and the species of mankind. As mankind progresses, the obstacles and challenges will become more dire. It will become necessary for more twin souls to incarnate in order to sufficiently deal with these changes. In the upcoming years, more and more twin souls will incarnate during this time and space to help lift the collective consciousness of the world. These souls may arrange any assortment of relationships with one another, including siblings, friendships, romantic relationships, coworkers, or parent and child. The type of relationship is less important than the quality of work being carried out. Although the aim of the work might differ, its intention will always be to bring about a shift in consciousness that is in the highest good of mankind and the world. Some examples of work that may be carried out include teaching spiritual lessons, performing humanitarian work for people around the world, addressing environmental concerns, advocating for the rights of others, and addressing problematic political and societal issues at the time. Whatever each group of twin souls teaches is exactly aligned with what they needed and decided to create before incarnating.

Twin soul relationships imply contracts that are agreed upon beforehand. These types of relationships are always divinely guided. Before incarnating, both souls went through a process wherein they decided the circumstances and parameters of their relationship in physical reality. What the souls decided to create is always in alignment with that which would bring about the highest growth and expansion for the souls themselves, for those in the soul group, and for the universal consciousness in that time and space. Upon incarnating, each twin soul then necessarily forgets the agreement and arrangements, at least on a conscious level. On an unconscious and soul level, both parties have complete aware-ness of the contract, but this knowledge is often obscured from conscious awareness until an appropriate time when the soul is ready to integrate it. Sometimes one or both souls may never gain awareness of the twin soul agreement. The amount of conscious awareness that souls have regarding this arrangement is less im-portant than whether or not the work between the souls is carried out fully.

Closely related to the concept of twin flames are soul mate relationships. The designation of soul mates implies a deep level of soul connection as well; however, there are also some distinct differences between these two types of relationships. While twin flame relationships are initiated with the intention of carrying out divine work together in the world, the contract between soul mates is created with the intention of carrying out personal soul lessons for each individual. Oftentimes soul mate relationships are romantic in nature, but again this is not always the case. Soul mate relationships may include best friends, siblings, teachers, or parent-child relationships. Soul mate relationships are less about fulfilling work together as a team and more about presenting life lessons that each soul intended to learn in this incarnation. For this reason soul mate relationships tend to be more short-lived than twin flame relationships, because once the particular lesson has been fulfilled, the need for the relationship is over.

Like twin flames, soul mate relationships are agreed upon beforehand. Relationships between soul mates also imply a deep level of soul connection. Oftentimes soul mates incarnate together to complete karma, or cycles and patterns that were seeded in past lifetimes. For example, a husband and wife soul mate pair may incarnate together in this lifetime in order to overcome feelings of anger and betrayal and to learn the soul lesson of forgiveness. In order for this lesson to occur and the learning to be carried out, the husband may cheat on his wife and create an opportunity to break the karmic cycle by providing her the chance to practice forgiveness. If the learning does not occur, or if the lesson is not integrated, the two souls will reincarnate in another lifetime and set up circumstances once again to provide opportunities for soul growth and learning. The longer it takes for a soul to learn a particular lesson, the more challenging the circumstances will become.

The lessons that soul mates come to teach each other are often painful. This is because they are the specific lessons that the soul needs most to expand and develop, and it is through adversity that people tend to transform the most. The lessons most commonly carried out in soul mate relationships include lessons of forgiveness (toward self and others), empathy, unconditional love, respect, healing, the release of anger and resentment, love of self, honesty, integrity, and loyalty. There are as many soul lessons to learn as there are souls themselves. However, in soul mate relationships, the lessons are deeply intimate and personal. A person's soul mate knows and understands that person's soul on a deep level. That is why there is often an intense pull or recognition between soul mates. They are the ones that you have been with time and time again, working through the same lessons in different lifetimes and different scenarios. It is the same soul in front of you again, only this time wearing a different mask. The circumstances of your meeting were agreed upon beforehand, just as were the soul lessons that you agreed to learn through the circumstances of the relationship.

You do not need to go and seek out your twin flame or soul mate relationship. Rest assured that they will come to you precisely when they are meant to. The universe will deliver them to you without your having to do a thing. Rest assured as well that all of the people and relationships in your life are there for a specific reason, a reason which you created and agreed upon before being born into your physical body. The reasons will all be brought to light in time.

CHAPTER THIRTEEN
CLASSROOM STRUCTURE

The learning that occurs in the physical world on Earth does not cease in the Spirit World. Indeed, the learning and the lessons continue, often to a much deeper extent than before. The Earth serves as one giant classroom, so to speak, much like a giant playground of God's creation in which souls are given an opportunity to expand, create, and work through lessons and relationships with others. This is one of the primary reasons that souls incarnate: to have an experience in form, within a physical body, in order to provide the necessary circumstances for soul learning and growth to occur.

When a soul departs its physical body and goes through the transition known as death, that soul returns to the Spirit World, where an inventory of the learning that took place is initiated. This inventory occurs in the form of a very important meeting with that soul's master teachers and guides. This meeting is not punitive but rather very loving and compassionate in nature. You may think of it as a life review, so to speak. The learning objectives of that particular life are reviewed, as well as the soul's progress or lack of progress toward those goals. For example, a soul that incarnated with the objective of learning greater compassion and patience toward others or in regard to a particular relationship would have the opportunity to review their progress in regard to that learning objective. Soul progress is not made in a judgmental manner but rather in a neutral way that takes into account the amount of learning that took place in an incarnation. In other words, the life review places much more emphasis on the karmic and soul lessons learned in a lifetime than on specific outcomes of situations. For example, it matters less to your guides and teachers whether or not you stayed in your marriage than it does whether you were able to learn the lessons of empathy and forgiveness.

The life review process typically takes place very shortly after a soul has reentered the Spirit World. There may be a brief resting and orientation period prior to the life review in which the soul is reacquainted with loved ones and friends who have passed on. This is generally a sweet and joyous reunion. Followed by this re-union, the newly arrived soul is greeted by its teachers and guides. Every soul assigned to a human body has its own guides. These guides are beings in the Spirit World who have agreed to work with this particular soul throughout its journey and incarnation on the Earth. The guides are always present, whether the person on Earth is aware of them or not. They are available to assist the person in a multitude of ways, ranging from planting certain sug-gestions in a person's mind to coordinating and assisting in the arrangement of circumstances, such as important jobs, meetings, and relationships. They are also always present to provide love, support, and guidance to human souls. Such guides have nothing but the purest intentions at heart. They are aware of a particular person's challenges and strengths as well as the lessons that the person intended to learn. They are there to provide guidance and support and to steer the person toward their highest potential on the Earth. Although such guides can and do fluctuate throughout a person's life according to their needs at the time, no one is ever without assigned guides and teachers in the Spirit World.

During the life review, a person's master guide is present. The master guide is one who has been with you for many incarnations and who knows your soul lessons well. Master guides have the benefit of having worked with you hundreds of times, so they know your history. During the life review, this guide assists you in the process of reviewing your progress in regard to the life lessons that you charted for yourself. If, prior to incarnating, you had decided it was in your soul's highest good to learn lessons about trust through the process of abandonment, then during the life review, your master guide would support you in looking at how well you learned this lesson in your previous life. If you had charted out for yourself lessons of forgiveness through the experience of betrayal, your responses in regard to those circumstances would be examined. Such examinations always focus on the progress made. The master guides and teachers are never critical or judgmental but rather are unconditionally loving and forgiving. They understand on a deep level the inherent challenges of being human, and they understand as well the specific challenges that your soul has to overcome.

The life review is not a process to be feared but honored. It is a great honor and achievement to complete an incarnation and be given the opportunity to review one's progress from a soul level. The ultimate goal of all souls is self-realization. That is, souls will continue to incarnate over and over until they purify themselves and are able to reclaim their divine nature. Souls reincarnate repeatedly, each time with the intention of clearing karma and learning important soul lessons so that they may become closer and closer to Source, until they are finally able to claim and live in awareness of their divinity while embodying a human form on the Earth plane. This process is often called enlightenment.

The joy is contained within the process and the journey. There is no point to rush to the finish line, because the journey is ultimately about the lessons learned rather than the outcome. All souls will eventually make their way to their destination because all souls are infinite. Each person must release judgments about their progress because each person is exactly where they are meant to be in their journey of becoming.

Even when a soul reaches enlightenment, there is continual learning that takes places in the Spirit World. The learning therefore never ends. This is why it is so valuable for souls to release their addiction and preoccupation with achievement. The achievement is not contained in the outcome but rather in the process of evolution and growth. In this sense, the process is the outcome.

Human beings are divine souls who are engaged in a continual process of learning, expansion, and growth. As a human being, both on the Earth plane and in the Spirit World, you never fully get there. You never fully get it all done, and you never fully arrive. There is always more learning to do, always more layers to pull back, always more of the mystery to explore—and how joyful that realization is! When and if a person does have an enlightenment experience and fully arrives, so to speak, the sense of arrival is nothing more than the realization that they have woken up from the place they always were. In other words, they are merely arriving and awakening to themselves and nothing more. They have gone on a journey only to recognize themselves *as* the journey.

The journey will only take you deeper and deeper into yourself. Each completed lifetime is like a ring around a tree. Together, all of the rings tell a story. It is a story of triumphs, of joys and struggles and fears. It is a story that never truly ends, although there may be new chapters that begin. The story continues on infinitely because you are by nature infinite. There is truly no end to your story, even here on the other side. Reentering the Spirit World should be viewed more as a new chapter to your story rather than as an ending to your story.

Entering the Spirit World once again truly is like beginning a new chapter. It is your home, the place your spirit longs for and knows so well on an intimate level. To make a comparison, it is like once again entering the womb of your mother. It evokes an instinctual, visceral knowing and familiarity that resides deep within your being. The feeling of being nurtured, comforted, safe, and loved is paramount here. The sense of connection pervades all things. Even though there are continued lessons and assignments to be completed here in the Spirit World, these assignments do not feel heavy or obligational in nature. Rather, there is a sense of clarity in regard to the purpose and orchestration of the lessons, as well as a sense of joy and appreciation for the opportunity to expand and grow.

It is this attitude of joy that motivates and propels the process of learning. Once they have been orientated back to the Spirit World and have completed their life review, souls are placed back within their soul groups. Once again they are back among souls with whom they have incarnated for lifetimes. There is instant recognition and deep remembrance between these souls. There is also typically great joy at the opportunity to greet the returning soul. It is a celebration and a sweet homecoming.

Souls within a soul group are vibrating at similar frequencies. Such souls are generally progressing in their spiritual evolution at similar rates and are generally working on similar soul lessons. Although individual soul lessons may vary from soul to soul, all those in a soul group may be working through lessons related to grief and loss or lessons related to anger and forgiveness. Souls are matched up into soul groups by master guides, depending on their level of skill, ability, and soul lessons to learn.

Much like in school on Earth, souls in the Spirit World influence and tutor one another, so to speak. There is a reciprocal exchange of information that occurs between souls, particularly when one soul returns back into the Spirit Word after an incarnation on Earth. Because souls in a soul group communicate through telepathy, there is an instant understanding and transmission of the information that a soul attained through that incarnation. It is instantly shared with the entire soul group. What is shared between souls are not so much the intimate details of the life experience (although these are available as well; there is no such thing as secrecy in the Spirit World), but rather the essence of the learning and lessons that took place. The knowledge that one soul gains is therefore knowledge for all. This is partly because the sense of separateness created by the development of the ego on Earth is not present within the Spirit World.

The master guides are there to assist souls in their learning process. They can be conceived of as teachers, much like teachers in schools on the Earth plane, yet their role is much more multifaceted and complex. The master guides are ascended souls who have held an earthly body themselves. Throughout their many lifetimes, they have ascended in consciousness and in their learning process and are therefore deemed ready to serve as guides. Souls within a soul group share the same guide while they are incarnated on Earth. The sharing of guides in no way detracts from the quality of attention, instruction, and love that each guide provides to souls. Guides are highly evolved beings who are able to differentiate their consciousness in such a way that they can focus their attention in many places at once. They are not limited to or constrained by the physicality of the body.

Guides assist souls in integrating and learning soul lessons in a variety of ways. Guides may instruct souls to continue examining particular life choices that they made and encourage them to think about particular karmic patterns that they have repeated lifetime after lifetime. Guides will solicit the help of other souls within the soul group by asking a certain soul to provide feedback to another. They may also create group exercises with souls in a soul group, especially if certain souls were incarnated together in the same lifetime. For example, if a husband and wife were a couple together on Earth and the husband died, followed by the wife three years later, both would be reunited in the Spirit World. If this couple were part of the same soul group (which they likely would be), master guides may initiate exercises or discussions between these two souls to help them continue to integrate their learning process from the previous life.

Assignments generated from guides are always loving and fair in nature. Such assignments are a reflection of the lessons that a particular soul is working to integrate. They are given with the pure intention of assisting souls in their spiritual evolution and growth.

Souls are generally very willing to complete these assignments. If for some reason a soul was resistant in some way, it would likely be because the assignment stirred up unresolved feelings for the soul that were experienced as uncomfortable. Souls do not experience emotions in the Spirit World in the same way that human beings experience them on the Earth plane. The primary sensation felt in the Spirit World is that of joy and unconditional love. Yet, just like on the Earth plane, souls are continually creating their experience in the Spirit World. They are responsible for the creation of their experience as well as the quality of their learning. Master guides cannot force souls to do anything, because in the Spirit World, the law of free will remains. Therefore, some particular souls may occasionally experience a form of resistance in the Spirit World or in regard to their assignments. Any issues or disturbances will be closely monitored by the master guides.

There is much joy at the process of learning that takes place in the Spirit World. Unlike school on the Earth plane, where learning is often viewed with resistance, in the Spirit World, the veil is lifted, and souls have the ability to understand the whole of their experience with total clarity. There is a lack of confusion regarding the purpose of their life and incarnation. All of it makes complete sense in the Spirit World, so there is no protest or resistance to the process. Souls generally undertake to learn their lessons with gratitude and willingness. How well souls progress in their studies and in their assignments will eventually dictate what lessons they continue working on in their next incarnation.

The classroom structure of the Spirit World is set up for the highest growth and evolution of your soul. Know that in the great classroom and school of Earth, you are eternally guided by loving guides who have nothing but your highest intentions in mind. Unlike the classroom in a formalized school setting, you cannot fail in your experiences on the Earth school. You will be given multiple opportunities to try again, if you so choose, until your heart and mind integrate the lessons you came here to learn.

CHAPTER FOURTEEN
INCARNATING AND CHOOSING A LIFE

The process of incarnation begins as soon as a soul decides that it is time to take a human body again. This decision is not one that is taken lightly, and typically the soul is prompted by its master guides that oversee that soul's soul group. The length of duration between incarnations varies. Some souls may take much longer to rest, rejuvenate, and integrate lessons in between lives before incarnating again. Other souls may require less of a resting period and may be ready to incarnate again sooner. Souls never incarnate into a body again before they are ready. A soul's level of readiness to incarnate depends on many factors, such as that soul's experience in his or her prior incarnation. For example, a soul who completed a life in which he or she learned many of the soul lessons that he/she set out to learn might have less resistance to incarnating again than a soul who experienced difficulty and challenges in their previous life. Many souls do find it difficult to leave the comfort and ease of the Spirit World, especially in comparison to the rigidity and harshness that life on Earth can bring.

However, it should be understood that regardless of the soul's particular feelings or resistances to incarnating, choosing a life and returning to Earth is *always* a joyous event. While some souls may feel anticipation or some nervousness about returning to Earth, the feelings of love, joy, and excitement generally far outweigh any reservations that a soul may harbor. Being gifted a human body and an opportunity to express oneself in form on the Earth plane is truly a miraculous event. Oftentimes, the spirit longs to express itself in form on the Earth plane in order to unite the substance of the spirit with the density of the tangible world. Although it can be difficult to leave the Spirit World and the ones in the soul group, the soul is comforted by the knowledge that it will invariably be returned back home once its journey to Earth is complete.

The soul must incarnate on Earth in order to practice and fully realize the soul lessons that it has been studying in the Spirit World. In the Spirit World, there is perfect clarity, order, and flow. The obstacles and blocks that cause confusion on Earth do not exist in the Spirit World, so souls know exactly who they are, what their purpose is, and what they need to learn to evolve and become more and more like the Creator. Therefore, souls know and understand the importance of incarnating. Souls know that the best way for them to evolve is to take a human body so they may know in an experiential way the lessons they have been studying in the Spirit World. For instance, a soul who is studying the lesson of acceptance and patience in relationships may understand the value of these lessons conceptually, but until that soul takes a human body and begins to engage in relationships on the Earth plane, such lessons will remain somewhat one dimensional and conceptual in nature. In other words, Earth is the playground in which souls can experiment, learn, grow, and put to the test that which they have been preparing for. It is much like being in graduate school and going on an internship or practicum experience— so is life on Earth to incarnating souls.

There is great and extensive preparation that takes place before a soul incarnates. Souls may know for some time that it is their time to take a body again. They will have discussions and make plans with their master guides in regard to beginning the process of preparation for incarnation and life selection. Although souls may be advised by their guides and peers in their soul group about when it is time to incarnate, ultimately it is up to the soul whether they will agree to incarnate again or not. For even in the Spirit World, souls have been granted free will. A soul cannot be forced to incarnate under any circumstances; they must consent to the process before it begins. For those souls who are struggling with the decision or who experience fears about returning to Earth, their guides are readily available to advise and support them in working through the process.

Generally, however, souls are excited and eager to make plans for their next life experience. Souls will meet with a panel of guides, which includes their own personal guides, but also other highly advanced beings who serve on what may be called a "life selection panel." These guides, or council members, serve the purpose of preparing the soul for its return back to Earth. Together they evaluate the soul's progress in its previous life, including major challenges, triumphs, and lessons learned. Similar to the panel that greeted the newly incoming soul back into the Spirit World after physical death, this panel assumes the responsibility of preparing the departing soul for its upcoming journey back to Earth.

This panel will work with the soul to outline and discuss major areas of learning and growth to take place in the upcoming life. Because free will exists, the outcome of life events remains open ended, for the soul must be given freedom to execute choices and judgment. However, particular life circumstances are arranged in order to best serve the soul lessons that a particular soul is intending to learn in the upcoming life. For example, while meeting with the panel before incarnating, a soul may decide with the advisory of the panel that it needs to learn the lesson of kindness and self-love. This decision might be based on difficulties from previous lives and other karmic actions and influences. Perhaps in past lives, this soul engaged in self-destructive behavior and was plagued by a lack of self-love and guilt. Based on previous actions, therefore, this same soul might elect to work on the lesson of self-love as one of the major learning objectives for its upcoming life. Therefore, this soul would agree to create circumstances and events in the upcoming life that would help to reinforce this lesson. Perhaps the soul would decide to set up the circumstances for a painful childhood in which there was abandonment from a parent or a difficult or abusive relationship with a spouse down the road. While it may seem odd to imagine a soul creating challenging circumstances for itself in its next life, the soul understands perfectly the reason for such events as it establishes them in the Spirit World. All of the events that the soul creates are the perfect learning tools to help that soul expand, develop, and learn the lessons that it sets out to learn. For without experiencing the hurt of abandonment or the rejection and pain of a harmful relationship, how could the soul ever learn to overcome such obstacles and develop the quality of self-love and self-care? The way in which souls learn on the Earth plane is through contrast. Souls oftentimes must experience the opposite of a particular quality in order to learn the intended quality: one must experience hate in order to know love, or sorrow in order to know joy, or abandonment in order to know connection. This is the system of learning in which life on the Earth plane operates, and souls are keenly aware of this as they create the circumstances of their upcoming life.

A part of your conscious, rational mind may find this concept difficult to swallow and may even experience resistance in regard to the idea that your soul knowingly orchestrated difficult life circumstances prior to your birth. If you find yourself experiencing this resistance, ask yourself: What is it about the idea that is hard to accept? What is it within you that rejects the idea that you are the sole author of all events in your life, including the good as well as the bad? Dig into it a bit. It is helpful to remember that it was not the human part of you that created the difficult scenarios: it was your higher self, your soul, that orchestrated these events.

Therefore, attempting to understand the rationale from the perspective of your human mind is like looking at the situation with a faulty lens. Your human mind may not be able to comprehend the reasoning behind the orchestration of painful situations in your life; however, your soul will.

It should be noted that while souls have the freedom to arrange the circumstances for learning to occur in their next incarnation, the events are not set in stone, because souls are given free will on the Earth. Therefore, incarnated souls get to choose how they will react to circumstances that were generated before incarnation. So if a soul decides to create the circumstance of a divorce in order to learn the soul lesson of forgiveness in its upcoming life, once that soul incarnates, it has the choice of how to respond to the divorce. There is no guarantee that the soul will learn the intended lesson. There is always space and freedom given surrounding the soul's choice in regard to how to respond. However, the lessons that souls do not learn in a given lifetime will inevitably be repeated again in future lifetimes, and the circumstances are likely to become more challenging.

Souls are given multiple—indeed, infinite—opportunities to learn the lessons they have outlined for themselves. In the context of soul learning and growth, there are no timetables, no judgments or expectations. Each soul merely progresses at the rate and level that is most suited to that soul, and no two soul journeys are alike. While at times there may be encouragement or a bit of pushing from guides to incarnate at a certain time, or to create a certain life circumstance, typically souls are so deeply immersed in the clarity of the Spirit World that they offer little to no resistance to making a certain choice or taking a particular path. Even if there is resistance, souls still understand the choices they are making as well as why they are making them.

Creating a life for souls is much like creating a work of art. It is, in fact, the artistic and creative expression of the soul. Manifesting a body and a life path is the soul's way of expressing its innate creativity into form. As explained above, this is done certainly for the purpose of developing higher consciousness and evolution as a spiritual being. It is done as well to overcome karmic lessons and to bring balance to the karmic energy. However, it should be understood also that souls choose to incarnate into form for the pure joy and adventure of it. That is, in much the same way that an artist delights in spreading paint across a canvas and creating images, stories, and shapes, so, too, does the soul delight in creating a new body and new life.

This is because the soul is created in the same substance and purity as the Creator. The soul is an infinite storehouse of creativity, and it yearns to express itself. Like the Creator, the soul is infinitely filled with love and joy. This is love in its purest form and is the building block of the universe. Within the domain of the soul, this love is so deep and so powerful that it overflows and yearns to express itself into a tangible form. This is in fact the main reason why souls choose to incarnate. Although all souls may not always be tapped into their innate love and joy in this way, such love is always present and remains the guiding force behind the journey of reincarnation and incarnation.

There is ample guidance given to souls throughout the establishment and creation of their upcoming life. Guides are always available to advise and counsel souls in regard to the life circumstances and choices that would serve them best. Another significant source of guidance in the preparation process for incarnation is the soul's peers within its peer group. Souls with whom a particular soul is closest know and understand that soul on a deep level and can thus serve as a valuable source of feedback and clarity as the soul prepares for its next life. For example, a soul who is preparing to incarnate as a young man in Texas with a disability may receive feedback from a peer in regard to what type of disability would best serve the soul lessons which that soul was attempting to achieve. This soul peer may point out that it would benefit the soul more to experience life in a wheelchair rather than some other type of disability in order for that soul to best learn lessons of humility, compassion, and self-worth. Feedback among peers is generally welcomed by souls within their soul groups. Souls can offer each other a great sense of comfort and guidance that is often greatly valued during the preparation process for incarnation.

Throughout this process, souls examine many possible life courses as well as different body choices. They may examine the possibility of incarnating as a man or a woman among other considerations as well, such as birth location, family of origin, religious background, and socioeconomic statuses. All of these factors play a role in the creation of a new life.

Souls also select their parents. Souls are encouraged to select the family configuration that best suits the soul lessons that they intend to learn. For souls who are intending to learn lessons of self-control or resiliency, they may select parents who abandon them or have difficulty managing emotions. Souls who want to learn lessons of freedom and self-expression may elect to be born to parents who are emotionally rigid and restricted in order to learn the opposite of that. And so on and so on. The particular choices a soul makes as it prepares for a new life are driven less by the circumstances it wants and more by the lessons which it intends to learn. The process is truly not about what a soul wants, but rather what a soul needs to best evolve and grow.

CHAPTER FIFTEEN

SOUL LESSONS AND AGREEMENTS

The reason why certain circumstances or people in your life may feel familiar to you is because you created the particular arrangements and circumstances that brought them into your life. Perhaps before you met a certain person or made the decision to make a change in your life, you felt a sense of foreboding or anticipation, almost as if a part of you knew that something was coming. This is because, in fact, part of you did. Your higher self, the part of you that is eternally connected to the wisdom of your soul, remembers creating such contracts before incarnating into physical form.

You have a contract with everyone with whom you are engaged in relationship. Some contracts, like some relationships, are deeper, longer lasting, and more powerful; other contracts may be more minor in scale. All contracts, however, were created and generated before you came into this life. All contracts were agreed upon beforehand. None of the relationships in your life, nor any of the circumstances, are there by accident.

This process is a part of the soul preparation and incarnation process discussed in the previous chapter. Once a soul has selected a particular gender, body, ethnicity, and family constellation, that soul will then undergo a process in which it creates binding contracts with other souls in its upcoming life. It matters not if some of the contracts are with other souls who are already incarnated on the Earth plane, because time does not exist in a linear fashion in the Spirit World. Therefore, it is perfectly plausible that a soul who has not yet incarnated would create contracts with the beings who will be its parents. In actuality, however, such contracts will already have existed on some level because the beings who will become the soul's parents will already have agreed to do so before incarnating. This can and does happen often. Therefore, it is important to understand that linear definitions of time and space do not apply to such processes as they unfold in the Spirit World.

"Contracts" simply imply binding agreements. This is an agreement that takes place between two souls. Much like the type of contract a person may sign when leasing an apartment or beginning a new job, contracts between souls simply solidify an energetic agreement that will take place in the physical realm. Because all souls have free will, both souls must agree to the contract beforehand. If a soul does not consent to a particular agreement, the contract will not take place. There is no coercion or force involved. All contracted parties must be in agreement for the contract to be valid.

Most of the contracts that souls make are with those in its soul group. These are the souls with whom you most often incarnate and are in closest relationship with. The people in your family, your spouse, and your best friends are most likely in your soul group. Occasionally a soul may make a contract with another soul who is not a part of its soul group, but this does not occur often. When it does, there is always a reason for it, such as the introduction of a new soul energy or a soul's decision to leave its particular soul group and join another.

Even though souls have agreed to certain contracts before being born, souls still always have free will. This concept is important to understand. What this implies is that while the contract may be in place, souls can still choose how to react to the particular circumstances of the contract. For example, imagine a woman who has recently gone through a divorce. She meets a new man with whom she feels an instant connection and attraction. Although she is not aware of it, she has actually contracted with this man before she was born. They agreed upon the circumstances through which they would meet, and they agreed upon the soul lessons they would help to fulfill for one another. They also agreed upon the potential of her marrying him and starting a life together. However, just because this woman contracted with this new man does not mean the full spectrum of possibilities within their contract will come to fruition. Because the woman still has free will, she can elect to ignore this man because of insecurities or fears left over from her divorce. She may decide to dismiss her feelings of attraction and rationalize the problem of getting involved with someone else "too soon." For all of these reasons and more, this woman could decide, out of her own free will, to pursue another path.

It is important to understand that in the case with the woman described above, the choice of whether or not to pursue this new relationship is entirely hers. This is because her soul was the one who laid out different potential realities that she could manifest in her lifetime. These different possibilities—such as whether or not to create a relationship with this new man—were not ordained by an omnipotent, controlling Source, but rather were created by her. As a sovereign and divine Creator, she created the different possibilities and potentials that she could activate within her lifetime, including whether or not to stay in an unhappy marriage or whether to pursue a relationship with this new man after her divorce. According to the choices she made, certain contracts would then be activated or not.

You may think of reality much like a mathematical equation. The variables are not set in stone. Because of the law of free will, you have the freedom to make different choices in any situation. Depending upon the different choices that you make, you will attract different potential realities to yourself. In any given situation, there are multiple possibilities that exist before you. When you select one path, it leads to multiple other scenarios and opportunities that open up to you based on your previous choices. So while you may create an infinite number of contracts with other souls before you are born, not all of these contracts are necessarily activated. Also, because of the law of free will, not every contract will be fulfilled to its highest possibility, just as described in the instance above. There is no judgment in the process, just as there are no "right" or "wrong" choices. If a contract does not get fulfilled to its highest potential, that is not a waste of that contract. It will simply remain latent, and the person will go on to fulfill contracts with other souls with whom they wouldn't have fulfilled otherwise if the previous one had been brought to fruition.

This process occurs constantly and is applicable to all souls. It is much like a giant chessboard on which all the players have been given roles and arrangements beforehand. Yet the outcomes depend entirely upon the moves which the players make. You are the chess player, and the circumstances and possibilities before you on the board were created by you for your enjoyment, evolution, and growth. The fact that you may not activate all of the contracts that you laid out in this lifetime is not the point; the point is that you, as a sovereign creator, have the free will to manifest a life that is in alignment with your sense of purpose, love, and joy. The point is that you get to choose what you want to create!

Soul contracts are always created with the highest good of all parties in mind. It is the intention of soul contracts to escalate spiritual growth and evolution in regard to all parties involved. It is true that some soul contracts contain difficult circumstances that reveal themselves between two or more people. Indeed, some souls contract to become involved in a painful or abusive type of relationship. Some souls agree that they will undergo some type of tragedy together in order to initiate or deepen a process of soul learning that would never have occurred without that event taking place. Souls may even contract to be involved in each other's lives in a manner that is less than pleasant and even harmful. For example, a child soul may contract with the soul of its father to experience abuse and neglect during childhood. It is important to understand that although it may seem otherwise, even the most difficult or painful of soul contracts are *always* created with the highest good in mind. Soul contracts that involve abuse in some way actually benefit both parties, because the soul who chose to receive the abuse has the ability to learn valuable soul lessons such as self-love, forgiveness, and the ability to trust. Conversely, the soul who contracted to initiate the abuse also has the opportunity to learn soul lessons such as compassion, empathy, and emotional self-regulation. This is not to imply that all souls in this type of contract will learn these lessons; in fact many times this is not the case. However, the opportunity for soul advancement is present in such situations for those who are ready to take it. For those who are not, they will continue to reincarnate and recreate similar scenarios for themselves until they do integrate the soul lessons they were meant to learn. This process can take many lifetimes.

It is not necessary for you to know exactly what your soul contracts are with all of the people in your life, although this can be helpful information to know. Especially in relationships where you feel a lack of clarity and confusion, understanding information about soul contracts and soul intentions for learning can be very beneficial. There are many ways to unearth this information, none better than the other. You may experiment to find the ones that work for you. For instance, during hypnotherapy, in past life regressions, you may access information about soul groups and soul contracts. This is because during hypnosis you are completely connected to the subconscious mind and possibly on an even deeper level to the unconscious mind. It is here where all of your memories of life in the Spirit World and the remembrance of your beingness before incarnation is stored. Whenever you tap into this storehouse of knowledge of the soul, you have the ability to access information about soul contracts.

Such information is also available to you in your Akashic Records. These energetic records are like the blueprint of your soul. The records contain knowledge of all of your lifetimes as well as information about contracts with all of the people in your life. It is possible to tap into your Akashic Records on your own in meditation; however, it is advisable to find someone who is trained in a method of opening your Akashic Records in order to help you best maneuver the information that you find there.

There are other methods of obtaining information about soul contracts. Some of these methods include exercises you can do on your own, such as using a pendulum and asking questions about a particular contract with someone in your life. You may also ask for information during meditation and in your dreams, or you may call upon your guides to assist you in understanding the nature of your soul contract with a person in your life. Regardless of the method you choose to access such information, it is vital to remember that all of the methods mentioned above do nothing more than reflect your own inner wisdom and knowledge back to you. For all of the information you could ever want to know about your soul contracts and intentions are already contained inside you; indeed, such contracts and circumstances were created by you. So do not expect to look to someone else for the answers. The most another person can ever do is reflect back to you your own knowledge, truth, and understanding.

CHAPTER SIXTEEN

DYING: THE JOURNEY HOME AND BACK AGAIN

D ying, or that which you consider the final journey home, is really the journey back to the beginning.

There is currently a great deal of fear and misunderstanding in the world today about the process of dying, what it means, as well as what it entails. Much of this misinformation and fear is generated from unreliable sources, such as movies, television, and the media. There is great speculation about what takes place on "the other side." What has been termed "the other side" in many pop-culture references truly refers to the veil. The veil is the energetic barrier that separates the physical world from the spiritual world. The dying process is no more than the process of crossing over that veil.

There is fear in many people's hearts about the process of dying simply because there is fear of the unknown. Dying represents the Great Mystery. It represents returning to the Void, into the unknown, into the darkness. Because the human ego fears the unknown more than anything else, there is a natural and innate fear of death ingrained within the human psyche. In actuality, this fear exists only within the human ego. It does not exist within the spirit, because the spirit knows no fear, and the spirit remembers the Void as the place from which it came. The ego, conversely, has fallen under the veil of illusion and therefore does not have access to the same remembrance that the spirit does. That is why the ego is often full of doubt and fear. The human ego equates death with annihilation of consciousness. On some level, the ego fears the end of its existence once the human body dies. This is a terrifying concept for the ego to bear because it craves so deeply the stability of the physical world. Entering the Void is an almost unbearable concept to the human ego. Even in those beings who hold a belief of heaven or afterlife, a portion of their ego often still experiences fear at the thought of making this transition.

Yet in reality, there truly is nothing to fear. The ego's fears surrounding death hold no weight; they are only unsubstantiated and fabricated projections of the mind. Truly the process of dying could not be sweeter, more joyous, or more comforting. Rest assured that although the process may look different for different souls according to their individual needs, there is inevitably great care taken to support those souls who have recently departed their physical bodies. The newly departed soul is deeply cared for throughout every step of the process.

Dying should be conceived of as a multistep process rather than as an isolated event that occurs instantly and is then over. Rather, the dying process is initiated oftentimes months or even years before the actual death occurs. Much like the process of pregnancy and birth, there are stages of preparation that souls take before the actual death event.

On an unconscious level, souls are preparing for their death before it occurs on the physical plane. Much of this planning and preparation occurs on such a deep level of consciousness that the soul is not aware of it; however, occasionally a person with a high level of awareness may intuit that their higher self is making plans for departure. This may even occur on a fully conscious level at times. Most of the time, however, souls generally remain unaware of this knowledge.

Although the steps of the dying process are not linear, they do tend to occur in general stages and follow a basic progression. Steps may overlap or occur in a multidimensional fashion. Typically, the first step in this process is that the soul makes a decision to depart the physical body. Because the soul outlined its life circumstances and events before incarnating, there remains a memory of the arrangements regarding the expected time of death. It is much like an artist who created a beautiful work of art many years ago and then forgot all about it as time went on. Many years later the artist glimpses something, an image, that reminds him of this artwork that he had consciously forgotten all about. However, the memory of that image remained ingrained deep within his psyche and subconscious mind. So it is with the agreements in regard to a soul's time of death.

The soul will know when it is time to go. The wisdom of the soul, when it is ready, reactivates the remembrance of the life contract that was created before traveling through the veil and into the physical world. The soul is often assisted in remembering this by guides on the other side. In meditation or in dream states, information will be revealed to the soul—gentle reminders and nudges to begin making preparations for departure. That is why oftentimes people may begin acting in ways that indicate knowledge of their upcoming death. For instance, people who are beginning the death process may begin to spend more time alone, or conversely, more time with those they care about. This process may begin to show itself as an inclination to spend more time outside in nature, to take up a new hobby, or to tie up loose ends in regard to relationships or career. There may be a deepening of spirituality where there was a lack of one before. There may also be an opening of the heart, a deepening of compassion and kindness as well as a tendency to take stock and inventory of one's life, one's accomplishments, achievements, triumphs, challenges, and successes.

All of these occurrences and more are indicators of the beginning of the death process. This process will look different for each soul that goes through it; the above descriptions are simply general indicators that the death process has begun and are signs that are often experienced and displayed by many souls. It is important to understand that the dying process that each soul goes through is as unique as the wide variety of souls that go through the process themselves.

The timing in regard to these events will vary greatly as well. Some souls who are in their later years of life may begin the dying process three, five, or even ten years before they officially depart. Other souls, particularly those who are younger, will oftentimes experience a much more expedited process. Those souls who depart suddenly will oftentimes display no signs of preparing for the dying process; but rest assured that souls who departed suddenly and unexpectedly were in fact actually preparing for their departure as well, just on a deeper and less visible level.

Just like souls prepare various possibilities for themselves in life before they incarnate, souls also prepare themselves in regard to their death. There is no "set" or "fixed" time of death or dying outcome for souls; rather, there are many options laid out before them. In other words, nothing in the universe is set in stone. Nothing is preprogramed or fixed ahead of time. Rather, everything is in constant motion and flux, just as it is in the Spirit World. Circumstances and outcomes are determined by a soul's choices and intentions throughout its lifetime. Depending on a soul's actions, different outcomes will be generated. In this way, human beings truly are the Creators of their own destiny.

Within that freedom, though, certain predispositions or likelihoods do exist. That is to say that although a soul's time of death may not be set in stone, there are particular chunks of time throughout that soul's life where departure from the physical world is an option. Before a soul incarnates, that soul will work with its guides to create certain "exit points" throughout its life. Therefore, there exist many options for departure, and when the time comes, the soul will select the option that is most aligned with its highest growth and evolution, as well as the growth and evolution of those in its soul group. This is not necessarily a conscious choice that the soul makes, although sometimes it is. In most cases, however, a person is not aware on a conscious level that they have selected a particular exit point. This selection happens largely under the surface of conscious awareness, oftentimes in dream states or in periods of deep rest and relaxation.

The soul will know when it is time to depart. Because the soul is infinitely wise and contains all knowledge and understanding, it has an intuitive knowledge that guides and informs it as to when it is time to return home. This type of knowledge surpasses the cognitive understanding of the mind. It resides in the realm of the spirit and is innate within every human being, without exception. Some souls will be more aware of this knowledge than others, but ultimately it matters not, because each soul is complete in its ability to discern this information when it is needed.

So, on some level, whether it be on a conscious level of awareness or a more subconscious or unconscious level, a person's soul will ascertain that it is time to depart the physical body. This discernment can occur at any point during a person's life. A person does not have to be old or near the end of their life to make this decision. It is a misconception that only older souls are the ones who are ready to die. Likewise, it is a misunderstanding that a person must have lived a long life to have lived a successful one. A person can, in fact, be very young, in earthly terms, and be completely fulfilled and ready to depart to the Spirit World. Age is irrelevant in terms of the completion of life goals and learning soul lessons. Indeed, some souls intentionally incarnate with the full knowledge and understanding that they will not live a long life, at least in terms of an earthly conception. Souls will agree to live a short life if it is in their highest good and in the highest good of those around them. These souls do not feel cheated or remorseful in any capacity, because on a soul level, they remember that they agreed to depart at a certain age. There is always a reason for what may be considered an "untimely" death on Earth, even in instances of young children and babies. While there are at times true accidents that occur where a person dies unexpectedly in a manner that was not laid out before that soul's incarnation, these instances are truly rare and are always addressed and remedied— for instance, a soul who lost his life in a true accident might be granted the opportunity to reincarnate again very soon after his death. More often than not, however, when a young person dies, it is because their soul chose to leave their body through one of the several exit points that the soul had laid out before incarnating.

You may think of exit points as possible portals between the physical world and the Spirit World. These exit points exist for each person as vortexes of time in their lives when the veil is thinned and the option for departure is there. For example, imagine being a passenger on a train. The train represents life and you, as well as the others in your soul group, are the passengers. Every now and then, the train will stop and there will be an option for the passenger to get off the train. The passenger, or the soul, may decide to get off at a particular stop; or it may decide it would be better to wait to get off at a different stop at a later time. The decision whether to get off or stay on the train is made based on several factors, such as the readiness of the soul to depart the train, the progress and attainment of life goals and soul lessons, and the amount of karma to be resolved at that point versus the amount of karma that remains to be healed and completed.

This is not a linear process, but rather a complex and multilayered one that occurs at various levels of the subconscious and psyche. Even though much of this process is usually largely unconscious, it is of great benefit to have some knowledge of it. Understanding the dying process as not so much as a separate part of life but rather as a natural extension of it helps to demystify and soften the feelings of fear and remorse that tend to surround this process.

The dying process is a beautiful part of life. It is as natural, organic, and as important as the process of being born onto the

Earth. Why should the process of leaving the Earth be viewed as any different? It is only because of the ego's fear of annihilation that the concept of death has become a fearful and dreaded one. Yet I am here to assure you that nothing could be further from the truth. Dying is simply the opposite side of being born. In a sense, dying is being born; the soul is simply being reborn back into its original spiritual form. It is the opposite of birth, where the soul leaves its original state of pure consciousness and assumes an earthly body. Both processes are miracles, and both processes should be honored and respected for the purposes and roles that they play.

Within my own dying process, there was very little fear involved simply because there was no time for it. Such is often the case with deaths that occur through sudden accidents (although of course, the event—which in my case was a fall—was never truly an accident at all, but was rather the way in which my soul elected to get off the train of life).

At first, I wasn't aware of anything except for the sensation of warmth and light. It felt as though someone had placed a warm blanket over me. However, my awareness was separated from my body to such a degree that initially I wasn't even aware that I wasn't aware. In other words, I didn't know that I had died. There was a stillness and a softness that seemed to envelop me from all directions. I was everywhere and I was nowhere. I was everything and I was nothing. I simply *was*.

Gradually bits and pieces of what had happened began to fall into place within my consciousness, like a puzzle being put together. I began to remember the "I" that I had been in my lifetime—Ally Willen. I began to recall the events leading up to my transition, including the hike I had embarked upon with my friends. As these events emerged back into my consciousness, it was as though I was watching them unfold scene by scene on an old reel-to-reel movie projector. I did not feel emotion as these scenes flickered in my mind. Emotions such as fear, anger, or grief were simply not relevant to me in my post-transitional state. Rather, I was keenly aware that the person named "Ally Willen" in the scenes I was watching was not me. The body laying in the water of the Young River was not me. A sense of detachment infused my consciousness, accompanied by a sense of deep clarity, understanding, and acceptance. I was continuously aware of a sense of warmth that poured over me as I processed what had occurred. Eventually— what could have been seconds, minutes, or hours later, for designations of time did not exist where I was—my Master Guide appeared to me in order to provide comfort and reassurance and to begin the process of acclimating me back to my home in the Spirit World.

I share this information about my own dying journey in order to ease any fear or anxiety that you may harbor about yours. In society today, death has become a topic that is viewed as taboo. My intention here is to demystify the dying experience and to shed light on what death truly is. The more that you understand about death, the less there is to fear about it. In actuality, it is not so much the dying process itself that is feared, but rather the mystery and unknown aspect associated with it.

Do not fear the dying process, but rather learn to embrace it as another aspect of life. Part of the reason there is so much fear in the world regarding death is because death is viewed as separate from life. This polarization of life and death has caused fear, because it is believed that once someone dies, their "life" is over. This is not the case, because life and death are not separate. Indeed, death is simply a continuation of life in a different form. There can be no disconnection from life. It is simply not possible.

There is an awareness and understanding of people's fears regarding death in the Spirit World. That is partially why once a soul departs its physical body, there is great care taken to support that soul on the other side. Although the process varies depending on the particular soul and that soul's unique needs, there is always guidance available from guides and other loving beings.

Oftentimes, loved ones and those who have passed before are there to greet the soul back home. No soul is ever left uncared for or unattended. Great lengths are taken to comfort the soul, although the level of comforting required depends greatly on the circumstances of the soul's departure, as well as the soul's level of readiness for death. While some souls require little to no acclimation, others require a great deal. Whatever is needed in the situation is what is given. Just as there is great care taken to assist souls in incarnating onto Earth, there is also great care taken in assisting souls as they return to the Spirit World.

A newly departed soul's acclimation back into the Spirit World will depend on many factors, but one of the most important and prevalent factors is that soul's level of remembrance of their true identity and their true home. In other words, a person who had fallen deeply under the spell of the veil while living on the physical plane may take a little longer to acclimate to their original state as consciousness without a physical form. Conversely, a person who lived in the physical world but broke through the spell of the veil, someone who already had developed awareness within them of their true identity, would experience less difficulty in reacclimating to the Spirit World. Often, these factors depend also on the level of soul growth and maturity. Older souls—those who have reincarnated into an earthly body many times—typically experience an easier time returning to the spiritual world because they have undergone the process more often. Each soul is always where it needs to be, and there is never any judgment or punishment doled out to souls. There is only unconditional love, acceptance, peace, and harmony given by those who are assisting the soul in their process of reacclimation and remembering.

Eventually, the soul will reach a point where it becomes reoriented back to the knowledge of who and where it is. It is much like agreeing to be an actor in a play, knowing that you will forget that you agreed to be an actor; then, after many years of being in the play where you acted in various roles and learned many important things, you step back out of the play. Sometimes it can be a bit disorienting to newly returned souls as they sort out and re-remember the details of who they are and what they agreed to do before incarnating. This knowledge was always within them, of course, but it became buried deep into subconscious awareness as the veil of the physical world descended.

Generally a soul's master guide is there to provide the brunt of the coaching and support as the soul goes through this reac-climation process. The master guide is one who has been with the soul throughout many lifetimes and so understands the particular lessons and habits that soul is working through in its life. Whether the person during their life on Earth had any knowledge or aware-ness of their guides matters not. The master guide is there to pro-vide support, to help the soul organize and process its experience, and to ease the overall acclimation process.

Once the soul has been sufficiently reoriented to its original state of being, and after the soul has gone through the initial intro-duction and grounding back into the spiritual realm (which also includes visitation and greetings from beloved friends and loved ones who had passed before), the soul is then ready to proceed to its next venture. When the time is right, the soul will eventually be led back into its soul group. This is also a process of joyous re-union, as the newly returned soul once again feels the embrace of its friends and loved ones in the soul group. Although other souls in the group may not have been present or made an appearance in the soul's most recent life, the connection between the soul and its fellow soul group members is nonetheless very deep. Always on some level, the soul was aware of their presence and connec-tion and love, even while the soul was incarnated in an earthly body. The soul may have communicated with members of its soul group at night in dream states or in other states of altered con-sciousness or awareness. Indeed, although the soul may not have experienced a conscious remembrance of the members of its soul group—let alone even know it belonged to a soul group—there always exists a remembrance of this close bond that transcends time and space. On a soul level, the soul knows and remembers its fellow soul group members and rejoices in the opportunity to be present with them again.

The reunion that takes place as a newly returned soul comes back to the Spirit World is joyous and sweet. It is filled with a deep sense of love, appreciation, familiarity, well-being, and homecoming. These emotional states are the closest that one could come to ever describing the sensation of being in the Spirit World. In the Spirit Realm, emotional states are experienced differently than on the Earth. Souls do not experience such a stark discrepancy in their emotional expression and experience. For souls in the Spirit World, their experience is rather one of flow and alignment. It is as if they are floating downstream on the great river of life. The river of life is pure love. The souls are carried upon this river as gently and eloquently as dolphins swimming downstream. They are completely one with the river; therefore, they have no opposing wants, needs, or desires, because what they want is not separate from what life provides them with. Conversely, on the Earth plane, souls are often opposed to the flow of life because they have forgotten they are one with it. Therefore, they may experience emotions such as anger, resentment, jealousy, or fear, which in turn cause them to feel as though they are fighting to swim upstream against the river. In the Spirit World, disturbances in emotionality do not exist in such opposition to the flow.

I tell you this so you may be comforted and understand that your loved ones who have passed on before you are not suffering. Nothing could be further from the truth. In actuality your loved ones have merged into the Great Source and harmony of All That Is. In truth, they never left it, but in discarding the robe of the physical body, they have reclaimed their freedom and ability to discover that truth once again.

For those souls who may experience more difficulty in acclimating to the Spirit World because of ties or concerns to those in the physical world, great care and attention is given. These souls may have experienced what they considered an untimely death (although in truth no death is untimely but is in perfect alignment with the divine creation), or they may feel remorse for things they said or did before they died, or they may feel concern about a loved one whom they left back on the Earth plane. Regardless of whatever the case may be, the soul's master guide will work to assist that soul and ease his/her transition. Although there is no true sense of time in the Spirit World, generally such concerns do not take a long time (relative to the Earth concept of time) to resolve. Master guides are able to address such issues and have much practice in doing so. So, too, do those in the soul group assist the soul in releasing whatever concerns that soul may have. Peers in the soul group may remind the soul of its intentions for the most recent lifetime, including reasons for initiating the death process. Typically, the deep sense of unconditional love and clarity of understanding in the Spirit World is sufficient to help remedy whatever lingering concerns a soul may have.

Once the soul is fully acclimated back into the spiritual realm and into its soul group, the process of learning and study can begin. Now begins the process of the life review, in which the soul is guided to review the course of its life, what choices it made, the quality of interactions and relationships with others, and the depth of karma cleared and resolved, as well as the depth of soul lessons learned and integrated. This process is *always* conducted with an attitude of unconditional love and nonjudgment.

CHAPTER SEVENTEEN

COMMUNICATION AND VISITATION

I n recent years, there has been much writing and discussion about the topic of the afterlife and visits from those souls who have returned to the other side. My intention here is to clarify any misinformation that has been provided and to offer simple, accurate, and reliable information that sheds light on the topic of communication and visitation from the Spirit World.

Rest assured that those whom you love who have departed from the physical world can and do visit you often. These visits often are subtle or etheric in nature. They may occur in dreams while you are sleeping at night. This is because at night the veils between the worlds are thinned, particularly during dreamtime. You may therefore have a dream of a loved one that felt "so real" because it was, in fact, real on some plane and to some aspect of your consciousness.

It is possible for departed souls to come and visit you anytime. There need not be a special occasion or day to warrant it, although they do tend to visit more frequently around events such as birthdays, weddings, anniversaries, and births. Departed loved ones visit and assist friends and family members during the death process as well. They provide a source of comfort and integration as their loved ones on the Earth plane begin their journey back to the Spirit World.

Departed loved ones can and do serve as guides for those loved ones who remain in the physical world. You may think of them as spirit guides in a sense, although their roles and responsibilities differ slightly from those of other spirit guides. For instance, a spirit guide who has been with you since birth would have a different breadth and scope of practice, so to speak, than a loved one in your life who passed on to the other side during physical life. The departed loved one may have a more narrow and defined role in your life, such as assisting you in developing confidence or moving forward and pursing a lifelong dream. Often the very roles and insights that a departed loved one provided for you while in this life are the same kinds of insights they will continue to provide for you once they have passed on.

It is possible for you to call upon and connect with your loved ones at any time. This is because they are no longer limited to the physical constraints of a body. The limitations of time and space no longer apply to them in their spirit form. Therefore, they have the ability to come to your aid, to visit you and check up on you, and to provide you with guidance at any time throughout your life.

With this being said, it is generally true that departed loved ones are more actively engaged and involved on the Earth plane for the first year after their physical death. This is because they understand the severity of the grief following their death and they wish to help alleviate that grief for the ones they love who are still in physical form. It helps and benefits them as well to remain engaged on the Earth, as it allows them to integrate their transition. Some departed souls may feel comforted by providing reassurance to their loved ones. However, it is true as well that a loved one's grief may be so profound that it begins to hinder the departed soul's progression. Your departed loved ones understand the importance of the grieving process, and they know it is a process that must be undergone, yet, just as in life, they do not want to see you suffer. They wish to come to your aid and comfort, to assure you that everything is divine and that it was their time to go. They wish to convey to you the profound sense of peace and connection that is paramount in the Spirit World to which they have returned.

Depending on the departed soul and the loved one involved, they will send these messages in a myriad of ways. Most of the time, they attempt to connect with their loved ones in the ways that make the most sense to them. For instance, a wife who died may connect with her husband who is still living through a particular song that resonates with the two of them and was played at their wedding. Or a young child who passed away suddenly in an accident may connect with his mother by transmitting to her his feelings of peace and joy when she is outside in nature or engaged in an activity that he loved to do.

There are as many ways that souls may communicate with their loved ones as there are departed souls. What is important to understand is that loved ones can and do continue to communicate with those who remain living after they have left. The degree of understanding, receptivity, and awareness of those who are living in receiving these signals from their loved one will vary and will affect the extent to which they receive the message. Generally speaking, people who are more open and who have cultivated a deeper awareness and understanding of the soul's continuation after death will be more likely to catch the signals and signs coming their way. Conversely, those who have closed themselves off to even the possibility of continued existence after death or to communication with those who have passed on will be far less likely to receive such messages. This does not mean that their loved ones are not sending them signs. It simply means that their receptivity to receiving such signals is lessened. This level of receptivity is completely and entirely dependent on the person's mind-set and can easily be changed if the person wishes to do so. The change, however, must be initiated from within the person himself or herself, rather than stemming from without. In other words, a person must want to change his or her mind-set and cultivate more receptivity to receiving messages; it cannot be forced.

To change one's mind-set, one must simply be willing to believe in the possibility of continued contact and communication. It is not necessary for a person to have experienced it or to have extensive, or any, knowledge on the subject. It is simply a matter of opening up to the possibility that such an event could be possible. Much like the lotus flower blossoming forth from murky waters, so, too, is the process of opening up to a new belief. Opening up to possibility of continued communication with a departed loved one creates space within you for the universe to deliver that experience to you. The only thing that remaining closed to possibility accomplishes is to ensure that such an experience will never manifest into your life.

It is entirely possible to continue to have and maintain a relationship with beloved family members or friends who have passed on. It is not difficult but rather quite easy once a little understanding and knowledge has been attained. Creating a relationship with your deceased loved ones is not strange or unnatural and is actually quite aligned with your true identity as a spirit. In many ways, the instantaneous connection, deep and abiding sense of love, and telepathic communication that can accompany such relationships between deceased and nondeceased souls mimic perfectly the types of relationships cultivated within the Spirit World. These same qualities can be found in the soul groups between peers. Therefore, creating such a connection is actually quite in alignment with your spirit. It is something you know how to do intuitively without even being taught. What is contrary to your nature is not connecting with the spirit of loved ones who have passed on but rather thinking it impossible to do so. This is a belief and trick of the mind that is steeped in doubt and disbelief, both of which are learned qualities. Connecting with Source, departed loved ones, and the unseen world are innate traits of your nature;

separating yourself and creating division and doubt between you and the unseen world is not. Allowing yourself permission to connect with the Spirit World is not so much about learning something new as it is re-remembering that which you have forgotten.

With this truth in mind, it is helpful to understand some important points as you proceed in your quest to connect with those beyond the veil:

- Everyone's experience is different. Because your individual constitution and vibrational frequency is completely unique and different from anyone else's on the planet, the way in which you will initiate contact and receive messages from the Spirit World is different as well. Therefore, it makes little sense to compare your experience to others' or to hold expectations of your experience looking or happening in a certain way. Remain open and curious in your exploration. Allow it to be an exciting adventure of learning and discovery rather than becoming bogged down by what it should look and feel like.

- With that being said, it is helpful to understand the most common methods of communication with the Spirit Realm: sensing, hearing, seeing, feeling, and knowing. Do not close yourself off to any of these methods, but rather be open to all of them. It is likely that you will feel most comfortable with one or two particular methods, but you also may experience several different ways as you begin to open up communication.

- Know that this is not a linear or straightforward process in the traditional way that the mind craves. You may ask for communication or confirmation from a loved one and not receive it until a day or even a week later. Or perhaps you receive the confirmation in a dream. The Spirit World communicates primarily in symbols, metaphors, sensations, emotions, and intuition. It parallels more the dream world than the physical one. It helps to keep this in mind as you begin your journey into this realm.

- Intend to connect with your loved ones from a place of love. It is sometimes difficult to do this in the midst of grief, for there are many emotions that accompany grief, such as shock, anger, betrayal, and so forth. However, the more you can intend to connect with your loved ones who have passed on from a place of forgiveness, love, and gratitude, the more powerful your ability to connect will be.

It is important to understand that your loved ones are continuing their journey beyond the veil. Just as there are lessons, experiences, relationships, and growth for you here on Earth, so, too, are there opportunities for learning and continued growth for them in the Spirit World. The learning and growth does not stop just because a person has left their physical body but rather continues on and even has the possibility of becoming deeper once a person is back in the Spirit World. However, just because a loved one is continuing their lessons and growth doesn't mean that they cannot connect with you here in the physical realm. Souls have the ability to divide their energy and consciousness once they are no longer contained within their physical body. When you ask for them, they will hear your call. Whether or not that soul will heed the call is ultimately up to them; most often, however, they will, as they are in a place of complete understanding, forgiveness, peace, and love.

Many souls wish and yearn to provide comfort to those whom they have left behind in the physical world, to let them know that they are okay, that they understand why things happened as they did, and that everything has a deeper reason and connectivity and divine flow that transcends the human mind—things of which they are perfectly aware of now that they have merged once again with their higher self.

Below is an exercise designed to assist you in connecting with loved ones who have transitioned beyond the veil so that you may know and have a glimpse of the perfection and harmony of which all souls are a part.

1. Begin by finding a comfortable and quiet place to sit. You may choose to be in your room or perhaps outside in nature if possible. What matters most is that you are someplace where you feel safe, comfortable, and relaxed, where there will be no interruptions. Make sure that you turn off music, television, your phone, or any other potential electronic distractions.

2. Gently close your eyes and begin to take several deep breaths. Begin to focus on the inhale and exhale. Slowing your breathing down is key here because it allows the thinking, egoic mind to relax so that your mind enters a receptive state in which it can receive messages from the Spirit World. Simply allow thoughts that come into the mind to pass through like clouds in the sky. Keep coming again and again back to the breath until you begin to feel a degree of relaxation and of calm. If it is helpful to you, you may use an affirmation: Inhale and think, "I am;" exhale and think, "at peace." Continue for as long as feels right to you.

3. Now speak the following intention aloud or repeat it silently in your mind: "I intend to call upon and connect with [deceased loved one's name] in the highest vibration of love and light, for the highest good and healing of all."

4. Imagine now, with your eyes closed, one of your happiest and fondest memories with your loved one. Think of a time when you felt connected, and loving. It could be a memory from many years ago or it may be more recent; it matters not. What matters is the quality of the connection felt. Envision that scene in your mind's eye. Allow yourself to journey back to that time and space. Feel the physical sensations around you; imagine the scenery as it was; experience the emotions coursing through you just like they did on that day. Repaint

the scene within your mind. It may be difficult or even painful to do so, as it may reignite the ache of grief in your heart,
but proceed if you can, knowing that your willingness to engage in that scene again creates an opening, a space for your
loved one to channel through to you.

If it is difficult to remember or think of a favorite or
happy scene, there is no need to worry. Simply imagine a
scene with your loved one as you would like it to be. Use
your imagination to create a scene in which you and your
loved one are doing something you would have enjoyed.
Envision all of the details—the sounds, the smells, the
sights—exactly as you would like them to be. It did not need
to happen in this physical reality for you to be in the feeling
vibration of the scene. You are the artist and Creator of the
scene, and your imagination is your medium.

5. Once you have firmly rooted yourself in the vibration of the
    memory or scene, ask your loved one to come in. Simply
    repeat, silently or aloud, "[Name], please come in and
    connect with me now. Allow me to feel your love and your
    presence." Now sit quietly and use your awareness to scan
    your body. You may notice sensations in certain parts of the
    body, such as the heart or the hands. If your eyes are closed,
    you may see an image of your loved one. They may show
    you a particular object or scene in your mind's eye. You may
    hear (not with your physical ears but with your inner ears)
    your loved one say something to you. You may feel sensa-
    tions, such as warmth or tingling. Or you may simply sense,
    through an intuitive knowing, your loved one's presence
    with you. All or any or none of these experiences are fine.
    Your experience may differ from any of these described
    above, and that is fine as well. There is truly no right or
    wrong way in regard to your experience.

    You also may feel nothing at all. If this happens, do not be
    discouraged. As stated earlier, sometimes communication

and visitation will occur much later after the request was made. This is because time as you know it here on Earth is much different in the Spirit World. Sometimes there may be a lag, so to speak, between communications beyond the veil. It may take a while for your loved one's messages to manifest on the Earth plane because of these differences. Or, your loved one may know that you would be better suited to receive particular communication in a different way, such as in a dream. It may even come to you when you are going through your day, least expecting it. Simply release expectations of what you think it should look like and be open to receive. Know that even if you feel or sense little, the intention to connect is powerful and may be affecting you in the deeper, less obvious aspects of your consciousness and your being.

6. Once you feel complete—and there is no designated time, for you may wish to sit and connect with your loved one for thirty minutes or for as little as three minutes—begin once again to take several deep breaths. Bring your awareness back into your body and into the present moment. Repeat the following statement silently or aloud: "Thank you, [loved one's name], for the gift of your presence and your love today. I know that even though you are not here with me physically, you dwell in my spirit and in my heart. I affirm our divine and infinite connection forevermore. And so it is."

You may practice this exercise whenever you feel called to do so. It will be different each time you practice it. As you continue, you may notice that you become more adept at understanding your loved one's messages and sensing their presence as time goes on. Much like anything else, it simply takes practice to become more skilled at discerning and initiating communication with the Spirit World.

Feel free to modify this exercise to be your own. You do not need to use the exact phrasing of the intentions and affirmations if they do not feel aligned with you. You may take creative liberty and change the wording to suit your needs. Connecting with the Spirit World is much more about your intention than it is about the specific exercise and wording that you use.

You do not need to be scared to connect with the Spirit World. It is real, and it is as much a part of you as your own spirit, your own heartbeat, and your own breath. It is here for you to tap into whenever you so choose, just as your loved ones are accessible to you whenever you wish to connect with them. If you feel like you would like to ensure and create protection for yourself before connecting with the Spirit World, you may choose to do so by envisioning yourself encircled by the golden or white light of God, Source, or All That Is. In truth this light is always with you because it is one with who you are. That is why it is not necessary for you to call upon it before you journey to your loved one beyond the veil. You are already protected; you are already loved; you are already safe. Nothing can harm you without your allowance or consent. However, if you feel that it would put you at ease or be helpful for you to call upon this divine light, you may do so when you first sit down and before you speak your intentions.

That light, beautiful ones, is always here for you. It will never leave you, just as the ones you love will never leave you but will always be an infinite and eternal part of your being.

PART THREE: INTEGRATION

AWARENESS OF BEING:
THE DISSOLUTION OF DUALITY
AND THE REALIZATION OF
ONENESS

ARRIVAL

AWARENESS OF BEING

The entire journey is designed to take you back to the
place from which you started, which is Love.

Purandev Speaks

When I was twenty-six years old, my sister Allison left this physical world.

When I was twenty-nine years old, she returned.

Her return was neither expected nor planned, certainly not in the traditional sense. At least it was not predicted by my mind. It was, however, foretold by a force much greater and deeper than my mind's limited level of understanding.

It was an ordinary Sunday afternoon when I came home from the grocery store with a pregnancy test. Having missed my typically regular period by four days, I assured myself that I was merely late but simply wanted to put my mind at ease by feasting my gaze upon the negative sign on the test that would almost certainly indicate "not pregnant." I confidently completed the test in my bathroom and waited assuredly for the single pink line to appear on the screen.

That single line never came: instead, there were two pink lines, although one appeared slightly fainter than the other.

This must be a faulty test, I thought to myself, and quickly reached for another.

Five pregnancy tests and a few frantic phone calls later, I was left sitting on my bed, shell shocked as surely as someone having just survived a hurricane, reminded once again of how swiftly the universal forces of change can tear away any illusionary sense of security in our lives. Images and thoughts sped through my mind at the pace of a freight train, expectations I'd had of how I thought my life would play out: having a happily planned pregnancy while

I was well into my thirties, when I would be married, established, and more financially prepared to bring a child consciously into this world; images of me walking down the aisle to marry my beloved in a beautiful dress—in my mind, the baby did not come before the wedding, for goodness' sake! My breath shallowed, and tears filled my eyes as I realized, as quickly as a comet blazing through the night's sky, that all the pretty expectations I had set up for myself were indeed as thin as air, castles built in the sky without any firm foundation to hold them up. All it took was glancing down at the positive pregnancy test in my hand for me to watch as those castles came rapidly tumbling down.

"It just can't be true," I said, more to myself than to my friend and my boyfriend sitting next to me. Both of them stared back at me, wide eyed. Their silence spoke volumes in response to my question. It couldn't be true. Yet it was. The double lines on the tests winked coyly at me, eliminating any residual doubt that yearned to cling in my mind: I was pregnant. Now. My twenty-eight-year-old, unmarried, ill-prepared self was indeed pregnant.

In fact, not only was I pregnant, but as I would soon come to find out, I was pregnant with the fetus that was destined to become the reincarnation of my sister, Allison Lynn Willen.

Ally Speaks
The decision to reincarnate again is not one that is made lightly. It is also not a decision that is made linearly and certainly not in the manner in which you are accustomed to making decisions on the Earth plane. The choice to be born again into a human form is multifaceted, meaning that before a new incarnation occurs, there is examination of all angles and possibilities of the meaning of the new life and the direction that it could take. All possibilities are considered by the soul who is electing to return to Earth; no stone is left untouched, unexamined, or unturned. There are guides and companions in one's soul group who offer guidance and support in this decision-making process. The choice, however,

is ultimately always left up to the incarnating soul. There must be, of course, consent on some level as well from the mother whom the new soul is incarnating into.

Although her conscious mind was scarcely aware of it, my sister and I had laid out the possibility of me returning in this manner, at this time in her life. It was of course not set in stone, because reality is fluid, in flux, and is therefore always changing; but it remained a potential that could be manifested, much like the seed of a bud that could flower under the right circumstances. Free will plays a role as well, of course; for my sister had the free will to decide whether or not to proceed with the pregnancy, just as I had the free will to decide whether or not to self-abort the fetus I had the potential to occupy.

In the Spirit World, all potential realities are studied and considered. All angles and sides of a situation are given their due consideration, but unlike on the Earth plane, in the Spirit World decisions are not made with the mind but rather with the wisdom of the heart and the radiance of the soul, for in the Spirit World, we are fully connected to our radiance. There is free will given in the Spirit World, just as there is on the Earth plane. Yet in the Spirit World, we are privy to more information, for there is no linear designation of time; rather, past, present, and future are all happening at once. Simultaneously, there are different realities weaving together in one continuous flow. Because of this, I could see what Purandev could not: the infinite joy that would blossom in her heart through the act of becoming a mother, the tremendous love that would be shared and anchored into the Earth through the arrival of this new soul I sought to become, and the countless lives that would be impacted and benefited by my return.

Purandev Speaks

Ally's death, when it happened, shattered my world into pieces and destroyed any sense of stability I had relied upon. Her return to this world, similarly, left me reeling with the same experience

175

of chaotic and turbulent emotions, like choppy waves on a storm-ridden sea. I felt like my life was a snow globe and someone had come along and shaken that globe vigorously, so all of the snow scattered wildly about, obscuring any hint of clarity from view.

"How could this happen?" I cried to my mother over the phone. Fear gripped me like an ice-cold hand pressing over my throat, restricting my vocal cords. "I don't know what to do!"

"It's going to be okay, honey," she said. "This isn't a bad thing. It's a big thing, but not a bad thing."

Not a bad thing, perhaps, but certainly a big thing that threw a wrench into all my plans. Once upon a time, my sister, through her departure, had taught me about the insubstantial nature of plans. Now again, through her return to life, she was reminding me that for all the plans my mind created for my life and how it was supposed to unfold, the only plan that truly held any merit was always the plan that the divine held in store for me. It was, of course, as all of life is, a matter of trust and surrender.

Yet I couldn't surrender some of the plans I had. "What about the yoga studio?" I asked my mother. For months, my boyfriend Alex and I had been preparing to take ownership of a small yoga studio in our hometown. Not only was it our dream but we both felt as though it was our shared destiny.

Like a movie in my mind, I watched as scenes unfolded in my consciousness of me driving to the studio, attempting to manage several teachers and classes, answering daily phone calls and emails...all with a tiny infant in a bassinet propped next to me. The air in my lungs suddenly had nowhere to go.

"We just need to see how things play out," my mother assured me. I gulped and swallowed a rock that had somehow managed to lodge itself into my throat.

The other plan that stuck like taffy in my mind as I tried desperately to process what was happening to me was the trip to India that I had been preparing for since January of that year. My heart was overjoyed with the opportunity to travel to such a sacred land

and spend time in the great Himalayan mountains that seemed to beckon me like great, wise sages. The thought of traveling internationally while pregnant, however, weighed upon my consciousness like heavy bricks. I had scarcely a month to decide what to do before leaving for the trip.

There comes a point in all our lives when we come to what we might call a crossroads, or perhaps it can be thought of as a train station with many different stops. At every stop there is a train that takes you on a journey—each journey completely unlike the others, each journey destined to take you to a different destination in your life. The choices you make at the station will determine how the rest of your life unfolds, for just like a set of dominos that fall on top of one another, each choice you make initiates a chain reaction that is set into motion within the rest of the universe. One choice activates all the other potentialities associated with that choice. It also affects the different people associated with that decision, thereby impacting their lives as well in completely unforeseeable ways.

All of this is completely unbeknownst to the average person, of course, at least on a conscious level—and perhaps that is just as well, because the pressure of being at such a point in life can be tremendous. The best that anyone in such a situation can do is to retract from the fear that tends to dwell in the mind and tune into the wisdom that is always present within the heart. Such a momentous choice can never be made with the mind alone.

So it was that with a tumultuous and chaotic clamoring within my mind, I was finally able to listen to the wisdom that dwelled within my heart center. The clarity came one evening when I spoke with two beloved friends of mine, a husband and wife couple named Patrick and Lisa. Lisa was, by trade, a medium and psychic channel.

She sat in front of me that evening, her eyes closed, as she tuned in to the energy and purpose of my pregnancy. I had requested that she do so, because my own mind was so cluttered with confusion that I was scarcely able to listen within.

"Spirit wants you to know that if this is happening, it is a gift," she said, smiling gently.

I said nothing. It didn't feel like a gift. Unless it was a terrifying one.

Lisa spoke again, on behalf of my guides. "They're saying that deep down somewhere in your being, you knew you were ready for this."

I gaped without speaking. Was that true? I wasn't sure. But perhaps...something stirred in me, a spark of understanding, faint but there nonetheless.

Again Lisa spoke, this time delivering the information that had been floating about in my consciousness, like an elusive feather that I could never quite catch ahold of:

"This child is the soul of your sister, asking to be reborn."

My eyes widened, and I opened my mouth to speak, but nothing came out. Instead, tears flooded my eyes, spilling out like bright diamonds. At last I had caught hold of that tiny feather that had been eluding me, preventing my full understanding.

When I could speak again, what came out of my mouth was simply "I know."

And of course I knew. How could I not? To pretend otherwise would only be denying what I had known even prior to my pregnancy occurring. For the spirit of my sister had come to me before, in dreams and visions, and told me that indeed she would come back as my child. It was destined to be, she said, as the two of us had agreed upon it even before we were born into this life. Such an arrangement was part of our contract together.

So of course I knew. My soul and heart knew all along what my mind did not.

Sitting in Lisa and Patrick's basement, my mind transported me back to one night months ago when I had finally gathered enough courage to share this insight with my partner Alex. Unsure of how he would react to such information—for he had never met Ally before she died—I nonetheless felt the impulse to share it with him.

Share I did. He did not seem very surprised when I told him, but rather almost like I was reminding him of something he already knew. It seemed obvious, somehow, like the final piece of the puzzle clicking into place.

After I shared this insight with him, he shared something with me. "Our daughter," he said, referring then to our future daughter who would be the reincarnation of my sister. "I've felt her. She came to me. She said her name was Madeline, and she had a light-pink aura."

Ricocheted by this presentiment that my partner had experienced over six months ago, I felt myself suddenly return to the present time, sitting on the couch in Lisa and Patrick's basement, with a tiny seed of potential being sown in my womb.

"Madeline," I whispered.

The time had come. She was here.

With this clarity came resolution. So even though, in the back of my mind, I questioned my sanity as I packed my prenatal vitamins next to my hiking boots, I prepared for my month-long trip to the Himalayan mountains of India at nine weeks pregnant. The picture from my first ultrasound stayed with me in my carry-on, proof of the tiny child developing deep within my womb.

As I carried this bundle of new life within me, so was I held and carried by the majestic mountain-scape of the Himalayas, vast in their wisdom and ancient knowledge. Despite my apprehension regarding traveling during this vulnerable time—not to mention my family's serious pleas to "*please* reconsider this trip," still ringing in my mind—I traveled across the world quite easily, by the grace of the guru. It was as though I was being pulled to India by some invisible force beyond my own control, a spiritual umbilical cord that bound me, the mother, to the lap of the Himalayas.

The beauty and tumult of India greeted me upon arrival. Secluded in the mountain ranges of Leh, Ladakh, in Northern India, removed from the business of the bigger cities, such as Delhi, I nonetheless experienced the myriad of scents, sounds, and various human experiences that lay like a tapestry sewn across the country.

It was a time of deep self-reflection, of shedding the old skin by which I had defined myself up until that point in my life. The mountains with their bright snowcapped peaks were everywhere I looked. They seemed to nestle me within their embrace, and they all echoed the same message back to me: "As you do the holding, so are you held. As you do the birthing, so are you birthed." Their silent presence reminded me of my own transformation that was taking place. Like enlightened yogis, the mountains simply were. They stood anchored into their sovereignty, unaffected by the change of the seasons occurring around them. They did not try to change themselves, nor did they attempt to understand or rationalize the events occurring around them. They simply existed in perfect awareness of their own *beingness*.

This message of *being* was transmitted to me during my time in the mighty lap of the Himalayas. It was the only message that I learned, and ultimately, it was the only teaching that mattered, for all other teachings stem from there.

Toward the end of the trip, our group took an outing to the Indus River valley. I watched as the setting sun began to sink low under the silhouette of the mountaintops. The mountains surrounded us in all directions like proud sentry guards watching over some precious treasure. When we arrived, the air was cool; the breeze was blowing gently across the landscape. Our group, over a hundred people from all over the world, huddled together in the mountain range across from the Indus River. The water was pure and clear. Stirred by the wind, tiny ripples on the lake were set into motion like little whirlpools.

Apart from the group, I stood by myself for some time, witnessing the scene before me. The juxtaposition between the sturdiness of the mountains and the fluidity of the water struck me as particularly significant, although I couldn't articulate why. The cool evening's breeze grazed my skin, and I could hear the rippling of the waves.

Without any warning, I suddenly thought of Ally. An image came to my mind's eye of the rugged New Zealand landscape in which she had spent her final days in this life. She, too, had traveled halfway across the world to a foreign land; she, too, had followed her thirst for travel, her passion for adventure. She, too, had found the courage to overcome fear of the unknown. Both my sister and I had taken the leap—not only of getting aboard the plane to leave the lives we knew in our own country but of finding the strength within our consciousness to grow and expand ourselves into something more than we already were.

"Ally," I whispered, "Sissy," and all at once I felt her presence with the strength of a freight train. Her spirit enveloped me. As I continued to gaze at the mountains and the water, I understood: Ally had seen this same type of landscape at the end of her life. On her final hike, she had been surrounded by the beauty of the New Zealand mountains.

She had fallen into water, and that is where the search party had found her. Water, the source of all life. Water, with its qualities of fluidity, of ebb and flow, had cradled my precious sister in her final journey home. Watching the movement of the water before me now, I felt something stir within my navel. A fluttering, or perhaps a reawakening. For as my sister's life had ended surrounded by mountains and water, so was my daughter's life beginning in the same presence of such beauty. A cycle was complete.

"Thank you," I whispered to Ally, to Madeline, to myself, to the mountains and river before me, to everything and to nothing at all.

Ally Speaks

The universe operates in cycles. Everything around you, including the physical world as well as your internal one, operates in a cyclical fashion. Rather than being linear, cycles are the mode of communication and expression which most closely align with the true nature of universal consciousness. All around you, cycles are an integral part of life: the ebb and flow of the seasons, the circular nature of the Earth and its orbit, the circular rotation of the planets in the solar system. Even the nature of a human life cycle isn't linear; it's cyclical. From being born as a child to growing up to one day raising a child of your own, the entire human experience is based on the cyclical nature that best reflects the natural pulsation and rhythms of the universe. As you go in, so you go out: even the circular, round shape of a pregnant woman's belly symbolizes the world's innate ebb and flow.

All lives and experiences are woven together in a tapestry that cannot be glimpsed with the physical eye but whose existence is real nonetheless. In the same way that the cyclical nature of the world can be glimpsed and *felt* within the structure around you, so too can this tapestry of interconnectedness be sensed. For the two are connected: because nothing in the universe is truly linear, everything and everyone is influencing everything else.

Although it is true that you are on your own unique and individual journey, you cannot separate yourself from those around you who have contributed to your human experience in some way. For your journey is theirs just as their journey is yours. You are a whole and complete expression of the divine in and of yourself, and that same wholeness is reflected as well in the wholeness of those around you. It is a paradox: you are both whole by yourself and also do not exist by yourself, for you are one with the wholeness that breathes life into being.

The cycle of interconnection is never ending and always expanding. In your life, you are actively furthering the expression of interconnectedness through your relationships, your choices, and your actions. Whether you are conscious of it or not, the tapestry is affected by you just as you are affected by it. No single action, thought, or deed exists in isolation without affecting the whole. In this sense, one person's journey is everyone's journey, and everyone's journey is one person's journey. There is no sense of linear separation between the two, for the time has come when the veil is thin enough to see that the lines of separation are blurred;

indeed, now the time has come to see that the lines of separation never really existed at all but were merely an illusion created by the fear-based mind.

Love has no ending and knows no boundaries. It is timeless. Love exists and transcends the definitions of time and space. My love for my sister and her love for me could not be quenched when I left the physicality of my body. It did not stop there but rather continued to endure beyond time. Eventually, the strength of our love led to the cocreation of a new life entering into the physical.

Love has the power to transcend any block, any obstacle, and any fear. Love has the power to reunite two souls who exist within two apparently different worlds, the physical and the etheric. It is through the strength of your love that you can call yourself back home to yourself, for when you are looking through the lens of love, you will see that those whom you love have never really left you at all, just as you never truly left them. Through the power of your love, you are one with them now, and they are one with you. Through the clarity of your love, you will see that you were never truly lost or alone, although it may have felt so at the time because you were viewing the world through the lens of fear and separation.

Love is the ultimate bridge between this world and the next. Indeed, love is the thread that weaves together the tapestry of existence. It is all held together by love. When you understand this, you will understand that in truth all things are one. You can never truly lose anyone, including yourself, because you are one with all that is.

I never truly left Purandev, and she was never really lost. Through the strength of our love, we transcended the polarities of "spirit" and "form" and met in the middle; and what a sweet reunion it was, one that had been awaited for so long, one in which we rejoiced in arriving again back at the place which we never truly left.

Purandev Speaks
Upon returning home from my trip to India, I occasionally asked myself: Why did I travel halfway across the world, while nine weeks

pregnant, and embark on a trip in which I couldn't take part in more than half of the activities because of my pregnancy? Why did I decide to place more stress upon myself and my family by traveling? Why did I do that?

The answer was simple. It wasn't to learn fancy yoga poses or even to learn deep and mysterious meditations. It wasn't to bask in the beauty of the Himalayan mountains, although I certainly enjoyed doing that.

In the end, I went on the trip to India to be. To be in the vibration of the Himalayas. To be in the energy of Mother India. To be in my own changing body. To just *be*.

As Westerners living in an extremely fast-paced and technological society today, we can find this a difficult concept to understand. To "be"? Why endure the hassle of traveling, flying, and paying lots of money to travel somewhere and not accomplish anything at all?

To the egoic mind, which is always focused on outcomes, it would seem that I had not accomplished anything by traveling to India. I wasn't coming back with a book of a hundred new meditations and yogic techniques. I didn't have a million pictures or souvenirs to show. Nor was I even coming back with any concrete sort of certification for my efforts.

What I was coming back with, however, was in actuality greater than any of those things. What I returned home with was not material things but rather a mind-set, a way of being. I came home to my own beingness, and in so doing, I came home to myself.

What greater treasure is there than that?

As much as our minds, our culture, and the world would like to convince us that life is about doing, this is only half of the equation. All of the doing and producing in the world stems first from being. There can be no wise and intelligent doing without first connecting with being. If you never connect with being, then you are neglecting the most sacred and fundamental aspect of yourself. All of your actions will have an automatic and frenzied quality to them, because they will lack the substantial weight of being to guide them.

Withholding any sense of being in your life creates fertile ground for the ego to take over and run the show. The ego likes to do; it does not like to be. This is because being is threatening to the ego. Indeed, being allows you to transcend your ego and connect with your infinite nature. That is because being is who you really are. You are not the roles that you play in your life, nor are you any of the labels you or others place upon yourself. You are vastly more infinite than all of that.

When you connect with being, you connect with the part of you that existed before you came into this physical body and the part of you that will continue on after you leave it. In this way, connecting to being transcends time and space. Being is the key ingredient that can bridge the gap between your spirit and your physical form. For when you dwell in awareness of your own being, you are aware of who you truly are even while living your life on the physical plane. This state of mind is called awareness of being.

Awareness of being brings you back to yourself and back into alignment with your true nature. When you abide in awareness of being, you realize that in reality there is nothing for you to do, nowhere for you to go, and no one for you to be.

In other words, you stop searching and realize you've already arrived.

Ally Speaks

In the Spirit World, we dwell continuously in our own beingness. It is the primary method of operation through which we understand existence. That is not to say that we do not continue to learn, grow, and evolve or that we do not complete tasks as you understand them. Nor is it to say that there are not designations of roles. In the Spirit World, I am teaching other souls as well as learning from my own teachers and completing assignments to assist me in my spiritual growth. But all of these tasks and roles stem from a wave of beingness that emanates from the great Source of All That Is. The waves are pulsated forward, and I am simply an instrument of the great cosmic flow.

All the doing flows forth from this place of understanding. All the doing is secondary to the being. All the doing is but a reflection of and in service to the being.

On Earth and while living in a human body, this is often the other way around: doing is given much more weight than being, if being is given any credence or weight at all. Many people in the world at this time exist completely unaware of their own being and will continue throughout their lives in this fashion. It is only at the end of their lives, upon drawing closer to the formless Source, that they may begin to yearn for a hint of their own innermost being, which had been there inside of them all along.

You need not wait until the end of your life to commune with the truest aspects of your being. Such communion is accessible to you anytime. It is simply a matter of setting the intention to do so and creating some small windows of space into your life to accomplish it. For instance, awakening half an hour earlier in the morning to spend ten or fifteen minutes meditating on your breath would assist you in connecting to your own beingness. It need not be complicated. Indeed, any stretch of time in which you are primarily more concerned with just *being as you are in this moment* rather than trying to achieve, produce, do something, or get somewhere, will connect you with the unending stream of beingness from which all life flows. Cultivating this state of mind through consistent practice is called awareness of being.

Animals dwell in awareness of being. Nature does too. This is why it feels so good to the human spirit to be surrounded by the beauty of trees, lakes, oceans, and shores. It is also why so many people find solace and relief through connection with animals. The natural world, in all its wisdom, dwells in beingness. The trees in a forest do not try and change into something they are not. They do not feel the need to produce a thousand leaves or to prove their worth by parading their beauty. The trees simply are. Through connection to their beingness, they undergo changes in alignment with the natural ebb and flow of the seasons; but nothing is coerced, and nothing is forced. There is joy just in the fact that they exist. That is enough.

So it is as well with a seed that has been planted in the ground or within the womb of a mother. A small seed of potential exists only in beingness. It knows nothing of striving or the pressure to preform to change into something it isn't already. It exists purely in a perfect space of creative potential.

When you can return to that state of beingness in your own life, even for brief periods of time, you, too, will connect with the raw, creative power of being, the creative power of Source.

Purandev Speaks

Both my trip to India and my spiritual awakening after Ally's death showed me that what I had really been searching for was myself. I had had it in me all along. And what was the mysterious "it" that I was searching for, the vague sense of something I had yet to find, the feeling that once I obtained it I would be complete? It turns out it was nothing more than my own beingness. In finding my beingness, I found the entire world. There was no longer anything out there that I had yet to receive in here, because I realized my oneness with everyone and everything. Finally, the search was over; I had arrived.

The sense of arrival that stems from awareness of being is akin to a sense of coming home to yourself. It is not something to be achieved through the mind but rather keenly felt through the heart. It cannot be attained through thinking; rather, it is a state of mind that must be *experienced* in order to be understood.

My awakening is not unique. Indeed, it is reminiscent of the journey that every human being has embarked upon. Every person in the world is also on this journey—the journey of integrating the polarities of their spirit and their physical form. It is not uncommon for us to become stuck between one or the other. Those of us with a propensity to leave our bodies easily and who yearn to connect with the Spirit World may be more likely to become overattached to the Spirit World and abandon the Earth plane; but the fact remains that we have a physical body as well as responsibilities and roles to fulfill here in this realm. Conversely, those who tend to feel more grounded and anchored in the physical may find themselves with a propensity to discard the Spirit World. This tendency presents a problem as well, as it overlooks the true spiritual essence of your innermost being.

As human beings engaged within this experience of form, we must learn to tend to both aspects of ourselves—the spirit that animates the physical and the physical form that houses our spiritual essence. Fragmenting in a way that favors one over the other is becoming lost in the duality of the world and forgetting the truth: that the spiritual and the physical are one. Just like Ally and me, they are extensions of the other, each providing a mirror image for the other to gaze upon so the underlying oneness beneath both aspects can be recognized. This recognition is awareness of being.

The experience of awareness of being is the bridge that closes the gap between your spirit and your physical form. Integration of spirit and form is not something that can be forced or coerced through the mind; it is something that can only be allowed through awareness of being. This is the primary work that human beings are incarnated to learn in the game of form: to learn to bring the spiritual into the physical and to recognize the physical as a manifestation of the spiritual. It is a matter of learning to look beyond the polarities that define our world and to see the oneness that resides underneath.

Ally Speaks

When you are incarnated in a body, it can sometimes be difficult to catch hold of awareness of being. This is because in your human body there are many distractions that threaten to steer you from your center: daily responsibilities and concerns, desires and fluctuations of the mind, and emotional turbulence of the heart. These concerns are constantly engaged in an ongoing pushing and pulling that captivates your attention. Although they may seem overwhelming and all-encompassing at times, they do not ever erase the essence of awareness of being that dwells in the inner temple of your soul. That is because awareness of being is as much a part of who you are as your unique fingerprint. It is not a matter of whether you have awareness of being within you or not; it is a matter of whether you can clear your mind enough from distractions in order to access it.

Awareness of being is like a key that unlocks the inner realms of your being. Through awareness of being, you can discover the hidden chambers of your consciousness that your thinking mind never even realized existed. It is akin to shining a flashlight into a dark cave. The flashlight brings into awareness new pathways and possibilities that you never saw before, because these possibilities were shrouded in darkness.

When you are living predominately from your conscious thinking mind, you are spending most of your life in the darkness. In this context darkness does not refer to qualities of "evil" or suffering necessarily but rather to ignorance, or what we may call "not-knowing." This not-knowing is the polarity to awareness. It is neither bad nor wrong in itself, for without the darkness of not-knowing, how could we ever embrace the shining light of awareness? The two polarities define one another.

In reality, however, it is only the light of awareness that exists. It was from and through this light that the darkness was conceived and born. This is the journey: from the original Source light of awareness, into the darkness, and back into the light once again.

Therefore, when you align your consciousness with the light of awareness inside, you simultaneously align yourself with the Source awareness that gave birth to your soul. You may think of it as a candle that resides deep within your being. This candle is never put out entirely, but its light can become dimmed through the process of many lifetimes. It is never too late to reclaim the light of that candle, however. It is never impossible to return to the shining light of your own inner being.

Nor is it a difficult process to engage. It merely requires the setting of an intention to do so coupled with the commitment to carry through. The inner light of awareness burns brightly within every soul. Its light can be strengthened through the healing processes of meditation, hypnotherapy, dreamwork, journaling, chanting sacred songs, and so on. The list becomes endless. What practice do you engage in that feeds the inner light of awareness within you? If you are unsure, allow yourself to become enchanted with the possibilities.

During my life in human form, I allowed this inner light to guide my actions. I did not always know exactly where I was going or what I was going to do once I got there, but I trusted the light of my being to guide me as I traveled along the path. The inner light of awareness always provided enough light for me to see the next step, even if it did not illuminate the entire path clearly for me at the time. That was enough. I allowed the inner light of my being to be my compass. I found it by listening deeply within to the voice of my soul whispering to me and telling me where to go.

In the Spirit World, the light of inner awareness is predominant within your consciousness. This is because there exists no veil of illusion and therefore no temporary forgetfulness. It is possible and accessible to see with perfect clarity. Once your spirit makes the decision to descend into the physical world of form, it knows that it will retain this perfect clarity nestled within its inner domain. That is why there is little to no fear about the process of incarnation: the spirit knows it contains an entire road map and GPS system to navigate the physical world of form.

That road map is awareness of being. It is your one-way ticket to your highest destiny within this lifetime, because once you are aligned with the light of awareness within you, it will inevitably guide you to your fullest potential and your ultimate fulfillment. It is more reliable than the advice of any person, book, or teacher that you receive. It will never steer you wrong.

You must learn to listen to it, however. More than this you must learn to honor it, for it will do you no good to excavate that light from inside of you only to discard it out of fear. This process can take time and may involve the releasing of multiple programs of fear-based conditioning instilled by society or by family.

The entire world is orbiting within the cosmos of your being. It is all at your fingertips, and you may access it if you are able to learn to navigate the software of your own inner light.

On the last day of my physical incarnation in this lifetime, I was hiking on the majestic mountains in New Zealand. My heart was swollen with tremendous gratitude and awe at the sight of such beauty. As I hiked alongside my companions, I experienced a sense of fullness and arrival within myself, the likes of which I had never experienced before. A profound peace washed over me. I said to one of my companions that I was proud of myself for living my life being who I was.

These words conveyed an even deeper meaning than they may seem to on the surface. What I was attempting to express was a sense of alignment with my inner being. That I felt a sense of fulfillment and satisfaction knowing that all of the choices I had made in my life had arisen from within the well of my inner light. In other words, my choices—where I went to school, how I spent my time, what food I put into my body, where I traveled in the world—had all come from inside of me, rather than been imposed from the outside. This sense of inner alignment unfolded into a vibration of joy and empowerment for the life I had led. My choices on the outside reflected the truth of my being on the inside.

It is possible for each of us to achieve this inner alignment with our own being. Rather than thinking of this alignment as a miracle of some kind, please consider it a natural and innate birthright that is yours to claim as well. You too can rest in a wellspring of satisfaction, joy, and contentment as you live your life in accordance with your awareness of being.

I give you the following exercise to provide you with a tangible and simple way to connect with your sense of awareness of being.

This exercise is meant to serve as a guidance system that familiarizes you with the process of connecting to the treasure within you. Once you have established that connection, it becomes easier each time you set the intention to do it again, until eventually cultivating that connection becomes second nature.

For this exercise, please find a quiet place to sit or lay down. Pick a spot where you will not be interrupted, either in your home or in nature. You may wish to have a pen and paper with you.

Begin by taking three slow, full deep breaths. With each breath cycle, feel yourself grow a little lighter and more present.

Once you feel centered in your awareness, bring the question "who am I" into your mind. While this question may seem simple, it has been pondered for thousands of years and has profound implications for those who meditate on it.

Keep breathing in a smooth and deep manner. With each exhalation, silently say to yourself all the things you are not—meaning those things that are not your true self: "I am not my job. I am not a wife. I am not this body. I am not these thoughts." And so on and so on. Continue this process with each exhalation until you eventually exhaust the list of things you are not.

Now take a moment and pause. Bring your awareness into your heart. Now that you know who you are not, ask yourself the question again: "Who am I?"

As you ask yourself this question a second time, feel into the sense of spaciousness within you. Keeping your eyes closed, begin to imagine your body as the solar system. See, sense, or feel the entirety of the solar system within your human body. See the cosmos, the stars, and the planets all orbiting inside of you. See the constant cycles of death and rebirth taking place inside of you. See the fullness of life in all of its glory unfolding inside of you. Allow the parameters of your physical body to dissolve as you feel into how vast and infinite you truly are.

Now direct your sense of awareness to the space around you. Without opening your eyes, imagine the walls of separation tumbling down and feel your energy merging with the energy of your physical space. Expand your awareness out in all directions and feel the breadth of your unlimited nature.

Take a few more breaths in this state, staying for as long as you'd like. When you feel complete, allow a response to your question to arise. Who am I? You may write your response down on a piece of paper or just hold it in your heart.

I am awareness. I am space. I am light. I am peace. I am that I am. Awareness of being is like a steady and reliable friend who will guide you to the truth of your being, over and over again. You may return to this exercise anytime you wish to connect to the sense of beingness within you.

That beingness within you is so bright and powerful that it has the capacity to dissolve all darkness. Resolve to allow that light to shine and guide you on your way. You are the way.

The way is the journey back to the self. It is a journey to be savored with each step, exactly as I savored each step I took on my travels to New Zealand. The journey must take you out of yourself so that you may find your way back in. The light of your awareness will be your guide.

May each step you take be blessed with graciousness and ease; may each breath you take be recognized as a precious gift; and may each pulsation of your heart sing in rhythm with the Source awareness that ignites all hearts.

Purandev Speaks

My unborn child dwells in awareness of being.

Nestled within the cradle of my womb, she is shielded and nourished in a sea of fluid. Day by day, her limbs and bones and brain develop. As she grows, she begins to move around more, exploring her surroundings by wriggling tiny toes and fingers. Sometimes she sucks her thumb. Other times, she takes a drink of the amniotic fluid. Always, she exists completely immersed in a timeless experience of beingness.

Pregnancy is the perfect exemplification of awareness of being. Developing babies, both in the womb and during the first year or so of life, do not yet have any expectations of themselves. They do not judge themselves about how they should act, look, or behave. They simply are.

In this way, Madeline represents the juxtaposition between spirit and form. Fueled by her own beingness, existing in nothing but eternal awareness, my daughter embodies and blends both aspects of herself at the same time. She is neither overly indulged in the physical nor attached to the spiritual. Rather, in her beingness she exists within both, perfectly balanced, perfectly aware.

One night in bed, I place both hands over my growing belly. Twenty weeks pregnant. My belly extends up gently, like a softly rounded hillside. With my eyes closed, concentrating intently, I feel it—a subtle kick as my daughter moves within my womb.

Instantly I see Ally's face bloom in my mind. Memories and images unfold in my mind's eye, like a camera roll: Ally as a little girl with wild ringlets in her hair, Ally and me playing outside in our backyard on the swing set, Ally taking pictures on our family vacation to Costa Rica. More images come, vivid and bright like comets in my mind: Ally packing up for college; Ally and me sitting on the floor of our living room after Thanksgiving dinner, laughing together at old photos; and, finally, an image of our family dancing at my cousin's dance recital around Christmas of 2014, the last time all of us were together in physical form.

I'm here with you, Sissy, she whispers clearly in my mind. *I never left you. It's me coming back.*

Upon hearing her words, I smile. A tear traces its way down my cheek.

I'm coming back to be with you, Sissy, she says, and the baby kicks again under my palm, as if to confirm the message.

In my mind I see the infinity sign, and I understand the message she is trying to convey to me: the journey from spirit to form, then back from form to spirit yet again. It is the eternal dance of creation. Done for no other reason so much as for the joy in the journey itself…just as my brave sister hiked up the stark and beautiful mountaintops of New Zealand. It is the journey of life. A treacherous journey at times, yes, with difficult and challenging moments to be sure. And yet all of it is part of the journey: a kaleidoscope of experiences woven together, intricately connected, held together by the thread of eternal Love. It is a journey unlike any other, and it is a gift.

We don't just go on the journey because we have to, Sissy, Ally whispered in my ear, referring not just to herself or the two of us but rather to all of humanity. *We go because we want to. And we don't just walk through it; we dance.* Another image of her flashes in my mind's eye, hot and bright as a shooting star: Ally dancing at a family event, favoring me with her best dance move, lifting her arms up alternately to showcase the famous "shopping cart."

Beneath my cupped hands, Madeline kicks a third time, drawing Alex's attention. He gazes at me, inquiring. "Is she kicking?" he asks.

I smile. "No," I say as a sense of peace blooms in my heart. "She's dancing."

And dancing she is—as are we all.

EPILOGUE
TWO YEARS LATER

Madeline Allison arrived into this world of form precisely on her due date—April 15th, 2018, at 10:17 am. Her birth seemed to occur outside the realm of time itself, happening quickly and also taking what seemed like lifetimes. After pushing rigorously for three long hours—feeling certain at some points that I simply couldn't exert myself any more—I finally cradled her tiny body on my chest and gazed into her eyes. Although it was the first time I had looked into my daughter's eyes in this lifetime, the connection between our souls was eternal and timeless. Meeting her gaze that day confirmed all the inner knowings of my heart: that our connection existed beyond the constraints of time; that we had in fact taken many journeys together, lifetime after lifetime; and that true love could never be limited by designations of time or space. "She's so beautiful," I whispered to myself, focusing entirely on her face. Nurses and doctors whirled around me in a blurry haze of indistinct chatter as they completed standard medical procedures. None of it mattered; I held the entire universe in my arms.

Now, two years later as I walk into my parents' house, the same thought enters my mind—*she's so beautiful*—as I take in my daughter's face in exquisite detail: her light brown, curly hair, full of luscious curls that seemed to have a life of their own. Her rich hazel-green eyes twinkle with the same joy and enthusiasm for life that my sister Ally's once did.

She barrels towards me as I enter the room, knocking over several toys in her determined attempt to be reunited with me. "Mama!" she cries, and I extend my outstretched arms, hugging her close to my heart.

"Hi, sweetie," I say, giving her a kiss on the cheek.

"Well, how come I don't get that kind of greeting?" my father says to Maddie, smiling.

"No one gets that greeting but Mama," I say matter of factly.

My mother comes to my side and picks Maddie up, running her fingers through Maddie's curly hair. "She's such a good girl. Aren't you, Maddie?"

Maddie favors us with a dazzling smile that could warm the coldest heart. The smile touches her eyes, which seem to sparkle even more brightly in the streams of sunlight pouring in from the windows. Behind her, a picture of Ally hangs on the wall. I catch a glimpse of the picture, taking in the familiar territory of my sister's face. The picture had been taken when my sister was eighteen years old, having just graduated from high school. She was wearing light mascara and lip gloss, something she typically never wore, being the nature-loving tomboy that she was. Nevertheless, her face radiated a natural beauty that shone through the lens of the camera. Maddie's face seems to emanate the same beauty now.

"She's the best," I say, and reach in to give her a kiss.

"Let me in on some of that!" my mom says, diving in to kiss Maddie's other cheek.

My father puts both of his arms around my mother and me, effectively squeezing Maddie into the center of the circle. Maddie responds to this gesture with a high-pitched squeal, followed by a giggle, light and etheric as twinkling bells.

I close my eyes and take a deep breath, drinking in the sweetness of the connection between us. *It's almost like the four of us are together again,* I think. *It's almost like Ally is here.*

In that moment I catch a glimpse of Ally's picture again. It's almost as though she is directing my attention to it.

I am here, Sissy, she whispers in my ear. *I never really left.*

In that moment, as I bury my face into the softness of my daughter's hair, surrounded by the loving embrace and presence of my family, I know that to be true—that, in fact, Ally had never really left us at all.

The Author in Spirit

Ally Willen was many things during her time on the Earth plane: a traveler, an explorer, an adventurer, a humanitarian, an activist, a friend, a daughter, a sister, and a (mostly) vegan—but perhaps most of all she was a lover of life. Ally's life was an embodiment of a legacy of love, generated through her desire to make the planet a better place for all living beings and through her resolution to answer with a powerful "yes" to every opportunity that life handed to her. Ally used to say, "All we really have in life are our experiences." In that sense, Ally's life was full of the greatest treasures of all.

Ally's intention in co-creating this book is to raise consciousness and awareness in regards to topics pertaining to the afterlife, spirit communication, and the divine nature of the soul.

If you would like to learn more about Ally and her continued impact and legacy in the world, please visit www.livelikeally.com.

THE AUTHOR IN FORM

Purandev Kaur is a thought leader, speaker, and channel who helps people answer life's biggest questions. She holds certifications in various healing modalities, including shamanism, reiki, hypnotherapy, art therapy, and kundalini yoga, all of which she weaves together in her work.

Through the loss of her sister Ally in 2015, Purandev was initiated into a deep healing process that ultimately granted her with powerful revelations about the continuing and eternal nature of the soul. Purandev shares these revelations in her Surrender into Being Masterclass and facilitates the Ally & Me movement, a social platform that supports people in healing from grief and normalizes the reality of life after death. Purandev also facilitates the one-of-a-kind Art of Channeling program, which teaches people how to channel and live their best life.

To find out more about Purandev and her work, please visit www.purandevkaur.com.

WORK WITH PURANDEV

Purandev Kaur is a highly attuned spiritual channel who guides people in how to connect with the world beyond the veil. Through her online courses, speaking, and various community platforms, she guides people to connect with the spirit world, heal grief, and live their life's true purpose. Her one-of-a-kind Art of Channeling program teaches people to safely channel different energies in the Spirit World for purposes of healing, growth, and spiritual evolution. She has experience facilitating women's circles as well as individual sessions that cater to the unique needs of the individual.

People choose to work with Purandev because of her authenticity, her deep understanding of grief as well as life after death, and her ability to create a safe and sacred container that unites people regardless of their background. Her training as a counselor, combined with her first-hand knowledge of loss, allows her to provide a unique space for true transformation to occur. Some of the benefits people have reported after working with Purandev include an increased sense of peacefulness in their lives, a greater sense of clarity in regards to their life purpose, and more understanding and connection to the Spirit World.

If you would like to work with Purandev or learn more about her offerings, please send an email to willenev2@gmail.com or visit www.purandevkaur.com for more information.

GLOSSARY OF TERMS

Ascension: The process of heightened emotional and spiritual healing and awareness, occurring on both a personal and a global level. The ascension process has been occurring for decades but is currently affecting people's lives at an unprecedented rate.

Awakening: The process of becoming aware or "awake" to your true self (i.e., awakening to the reality beyond the illusion of form and discovering who you truly are: a soul occupying a physical body). The process of awakening seldom happens overnight (although in some cases, it can happen spontaneously); however, most often it is an organic, ongoing process that can take weeks, months, or even years to unfold. Even then, because there are always deeper levels of consciousness to explore, we are never truly "done" with our awakening.

Awareness of being: A meditative state of mind in which you *witness* your own essence and your beingness; the eternal aspect of yourself that exists beyond all thought and physical form. Awareness of being is the state of consciousness that allows you to integrate the polarities of spirit and form.

Being: The part of yourself that exists beyond time and space.

Collective consciousness: The collective psyches of all the men, women, and children on the planet; includes all who ever have been and all who ever will be.

Consciousness: The aspect of one's psyche that is aware; the witness who sees the thoughts, experiences, and emotions but is not defined by them.

Duality: A fragmentation, or splitting, of the original primal essence into apparent opposites: for example, day and night, hot and cold, man and woman.

Ego: The aspect of one's psyche that is identified and defines itself through thoughts, roles, and memories; the "you" that you have been programmed to think you are.

Incarnation: The decision of a soul to become embodied in a physical form. For instance, your soul chose this particular body and set of circumstances in this incarnation.

Karma: One of the universal laws, the law of karma exists to bring balance to what has previously been imbalanced. A universal concept rather than a religious one, karma is neutral and refers to lessons of soul growth and evolution (i.e., "It was his karma in this life to learn lessons of forgiveness.")

Manifestation: The innate ability to create events, circumstances, and relationships through one's intention and attention to a desired outcome. For example, "She manifested a loving relationship in her life through her attention to the qualities she wanted in a partner."

Materialization: One step further than manifestation, *materialization* refers to an effortless pattern of attraction that occurs when a person is in alignment with the truth of their divinity and lives with a remembrance of their truth as a Creator. In this space, materialization becomes nearly automatic: "Because she understood her power as a divine Creator, she materialized the resources she needed to begin her own business without delay."

Oneness: The understanding that all people, animals, and places stem from one Source and, despite apparent separateness, still maintain an unchangeable connection to one another.

Polarities: The illusion of apparent separateness created by the ego. The polarities are the result of duality, and they exist to create contrast in order for us to know ourselves. For example, if we didn't know darkness, we could never know light.

Realm: Various planes of existence are designated and classified according to different realms (i.e., the "physical" realm on Earth versus the "spirit" realm).

Spirit: The aspect of our being that continues on after death of the physical body.

Spirit guides: Loving beings who look out for us and provide support and guidance from the Spirit World. Spirit guides can include deceased relatives, past life relationships, soul group connections, and even animals.

Spirit World: The plane of reality in which existence is nonphysical; a loving and welcoming place to which souls return once they leave the physical body and from which souls leave to experience life on Earth.

Soul groups: Clusters of groups that soul "peers" return to after life on Earth in order to learn and review their previous lives and make plans for their upcoming lives. Soul groups vary in number but typically include the people in your life to whom you were closest.

Soul lessons: Lessons that a person's soul is contracted to learn in this life. Soul lessons vary according to the individual but generally include themes of self-love, acceptance, forgiveness, and trust.

Twin flames: Two souls who have formed a very close relationship through many past lives and who have contracted to come together in this life to create and manifest for the higher good and evolution of humanity.

The Veil: The boundary that separates the physical world on Earth from the Spirit World.